The Way of
the Mother

THE WAY OF
THE MOTHER

The Lost Journey of
the Feminine

Carol Wallas LaChance

ELEMENT
Rockport, Massachusetts ● Shaftesbury, Dorset

© Carol Wallas LaChance 1991

Published in the U.S.A. in 1991 by
Element Inc
42 Broadway, Rockport, MA 01966

Published in Great Britain in 1991 by
Element Books Limited
Longmead, Shaftesbury, Dorset

Designed by Nancy Lawrence
Cover designed by Max Fairbrother
Phototypeset by Intype Ltd, London

Printed and bound in the United States of America by
Edwards Brothers Inc.

Library of Congress Catalog Card Number available

British Library Cataloguing in Publication Data

LaChance, Carol Wallas
The way of the mother : the lost journey
of the feminine.
I. Title
306.8743

ISBN 1-85230-267-4

For Albert
my chosen companion on the journey
and
for Rebecca and Kateri

"You are precious in my eyes . . .
and I love you."
Isaiah 43:4

CONTENTS

ACKNOWLEDGMENTS

I would like to thank the following people whose love and support was invaluable during the writing of this book. My mother for her faithful struggle and my father for his honesty. My brother, Andrew for financial support, my brothers Nigel and Patrick, and my sister, Sally, for sharing her journey.

I also wish to thank Stanley, Marlene, Bob Sevigny, Lex, Gerry Agnes, and the many friends who shared themselves so openly and authentically. I also offer these pages in memory of my friend, Pam Bergeron, who truly walked the way of the mother.

The work of Rosemary Haughton, Mary Rosera Joyce, Marion Woodman, Linda Schierse Leonard, Mary Neill and Rhonda Chervin challenged and influenced me. I thank them for their gifts of insight into the feminine. Thanks to my editor, Richard Payne, and all those friends who read and commented on the manuscript.

My deepest thanks go to my husband, Albert, friend of my heart, and to my daughters, Rebecca and Kateri, flesh of our flesh, for the merciful gift of laughter.

PREFACE

What would happen if one woman told the truth about her life?
The world would split open.[1]

Muriel Rukeyser

"Be a mother!" I jumped and looked around. Was there someone speaking to me? No, I was meditating quietly in the garden. From the rocking chair I sensed the almond tree swaying gently in the wind. I breathed more deeply letting my mind sink into a greater stillness. "Be a mother!" The words whispered again, almost too softly to hear. A deep calm flowed through my body. I breathed a physical sigh of relief that at last the words were heard.

I opened my eyes. Becky, at two years old, was absorbed in making houses for her friends, the snails. With exquisite gentleness she built them mud beds and gave them baths, or watched delightedly as they moved across the concrete leaving silver trails behind them. I smiled at my daughter, the one who had bestowed motherhood upon me. Of course, the words were true. Here was the way I had chosen, being a mother. The sun was shining, the air was clear and crisp, the grass still green, the nuts abundant on the tree. The whole scene hung suspended in a moment of timeless clarity. Everything within and without witnessed my emphatic "Yes" in response to those three small words.

In that moment the seed of this book was planted. Its germination and growth have required a long and patient gestation. I did not know how to be a mother; I am learning. I wanted a way as a mother that was different than that which my mother had walked. The definitions offered me by society seemed at best confusing, at worst completely contradictory to my deepest feelings and needs. I wanted to find a way for myself, a life journey, which resonated with my deepest longing.

The phrase which grounds my way is "pondering in the heart." The words "be a mother" came from a place deep inside me. The first step was to learn to listen. The second step was to learn to trust. The third step was to learn to wait. Two years later, in a different part of the world, I began to write. The writing was a way to articulate the pondering, to let the heart speak its pain and its hope.

The way of the mother is a profound journey. In our times it is becoming the lost journey of the feminine. There are no honors, there is no prestige, no genuine support for motherhood as a vocation. No financial rewards are given by society to the women who nurture the future. No emotional support is given to the women who are called on emotionally day and night, unless they are fortunate enough to have husbands and friends who value their contribution. No intellectual stimulation is offered to the women who are the primary educators of children. No spiritual vocation is clearly defined within the religious institutions to provide dignity and validation to the women who raise up on earth the Body of Christ. Is it any wonder that women seek more validating and fulfilling ways of being in our world?

Yet my experience tells me that the deepest longings of the feminine are not met in these ways. Woman is potentially mother. Not only mother of physical offspring, but mother to life in all its facets — intellectual, emotional and spiritual. To reject the mother in ourselves is to reject ourselves. To embrace the mother in ourselves is to become truly ourselves. To be mother is to be in touch with our true creative power whether we manifest that creativity in children, in ideas, in work, in feeling, or in vision.

My gratitude for the feminine journey as mother is deep. In this book I share with you, the reader, the stories, the experiences and the circular paths which the way of the mother reveals. The way begins with my motherhood, the experience of giving birth. The way embraces my relationship with my mother and heals the wounds between us. The way unites me with my spiritual mother, and provides me with a vision. The way reunites me with my mother the earth, and roots me in her body. The way reveals my mother, God, and teaches me wisdom. The way leads me back to my childhood, inward to my God and outward to my husband, my children, my community and our common home, the planet. The way roots me in the past, centers me in the present, and empowers me for the future. If my sharing resonates with you and the mother within you, then I rejoice. The feminine power of the mother has the potential to renew the life of earth and of heaven. May her wisdom be with you.

INTRODUCTION

In moments of confusion, such as the present, we are not left simply to our own rational contrivances. We are supported by the ultimate powers of the universe as these make themselves present to us through the spontaneities within our own being. We need only become sensitized to these spontaneities, not with a naive simplicity but with critical appreciation . . .

In relation to the earth we have been autistic for centuries. Only now have we begun to listen with some attention and with a willingness to respond to the demands of the earth that we cease our industrial assault, that we abandon our inner rage against the condition of our earthly existence, that we renew our human participation in the grand liturgy of the universe itself.[1]

Fr. Thomas Berry

Just as the seedling, newly ejected from its pod, enters the world in the assurance that it will contain soil, so the infant, expelled from the womb, approaches life on the assumption that it will provide a mother; for the mother is to the child what "mother earth" is to the seed; without her it would perish.[2]

Dr. Anthony Stevens

When woman lost her friendship with the earth, and with the universe, she lost a deep part of herself; she lost the mother of nature's beings . . . When woman regains her communion with the world, and when she educates the human family in this communion, her cosmic purpose will be fulfilled.[3]

Mary Rosera Joyce

* * *

She was just a woman. I vividly remember the moment I first saw her that way. Something opened inside me — a new possibility, a

dream, a different kind of hope. I just stared at her face and sat
quietly. It was a mild winter day, the earth still green and glowing
even in her dead season. I was sitting on a wooden bench trying
to come to terms with the amount of fear and turmoil I was in,
wondering whether I was mad or entering into something new.
I saw them out of the corner of my eye. She did not look at me,
transfixed as she was on the older woman before her. Her face
mirrored my inner longing, full of an innocent pleading, as
though she could wrest from that wrinkled face in front of her
the words she so desperately needed to hear.

The place was empty and cold and quiet. Silently I watched the
moment of their interaction caught in time before me. I felt I was
watching a play. In it I was an unseen observer presented with
a truth that even as I tried to grasp it, slipped away — as a cobweb
disappears through my fingers when I try to touch it. All I could
sense was that the relationship between these two women whispered something to me about what it means to be woman, to be
mother. The faces in front of me were etched on my heart.

Both women were with child. The older one, rounded and full
with new life, looked stern. I could scarcely see the womb presence in the young woman who waited before her. It was only in
her face, an anxious knowing in her eyes, hoping for celebration,
crying out for affirmation. In that moment my heart opened in
love. Even with all I knew of her, I saw her in a new way. I
embraced her as a woman with a love that has never changed.
In seeing her vulnerability and her neediness, I glimpsed her
strength. She had a dignity and a presence unlike any I had
experienced, and I knew that was what I wanted. I wanted to
interrupt the exchange, to run and tell the older woman to give
her what she needed, to embrace her as she was and to celebrate
this child to be. But all I could do was wait and watch the poignant
expectation of the moment with trust. That young woman's neediness gave me permission to uncover my own. Inside, regardless
of who she became, there remained a fragile trembling child
asking for love and acceptance.

I know her now in a new way. I have always known her story,
the events of her life, the mother she became. Yet today she is
present to me, available as woman and mother. In her everything
seems to be held together and contained. The paradoxes of life:
birth and death, beauty and terror, creativity and despair, related-

ness and aloneness, wisdom and unknowing, all melt into her being. She simply lets them fill her, offering no resistance, allowing them to be.

As I write, the day is grey and dark much like that day long ago. Rain pours down soaking the pine trees and the dying earth. Again it is the beginning of winter, a time of empty, cold waiting. A time for going within. But there is a luxury in the smells and the sounds of the day. The manure pile steams busily, preparing itself to fructify our soil. The sound of rain is a comfort with its promise of living water. The grey mist hangs suspended over every branch and blade giving a fairy tale atmosphere to the place. How beautiful the earth is in all her seasons.

This is my home. This earth fed that young woman from her soils just as she feeds me. It was her home too. Our stories and our dreams begin and end in the same dust. The ground my feet touch is common ground, for her feet caressed the dirt of many miles on her earth journey. She quenched her thirst with the waters which still flow today. She breathed the life-giving air more deeply when she was with child. Perhaps she remembers, as I do, the laughter of those ravenous inhalations of oxygen which so mysteriously nourish two living bodies. I am one with her through, with, and in our living experience of the earth. Her life is present to me in every sound and smell. She whispers in the sound of the rain and smiles in the sun's warmth. I am the earth's child, just as she was. As women, we contain the seeds of birth and death, beauty and terror, creativity and despair, relatedness and aloneness, wisdom and unknowing. The earth in turn contains us, she gives us life and takes us back in death. She nourishes our lives' journeys. The earth is our shared mother.

I am afraid for this mother earth. The news of the earth story is not good. As I watch the winter mist cover the land, it becomes a death shroud, not a fairy-tale. My heart aches. How many springs does the earth have left? How much longer can we degrade her body before she dies as a birthing mother and stops giving life? How will her story end?

I have two daughters. If they are to become women who walk their own journeys and dream their own dreams, they need a loving mother. They need a woman to inspire them, as the woman I write for has inspired me. Most of all they need a place where they can journey. They need the earth.

This book is written in response to the young mother I met that winter day long ago. It springs from the love and gratitude I have for her and for our shared mother, the earth. The life of that young woman teaches me about the feminine journey. She encourages me to trust my own dreams and to live them, because she trusted and lived hers. Her story is well known. It is time now to tell my own.

CHAPTER ONE

Birth
The Embodiment of Love

Woman's consciousness of birth, its meaning, and its echoes of
cosmic patterns is an unconscious, nonimagistic, nonverbal, yet
shared feminine metaphysic.[1]

Stephanie Demetrakopoulos

First, I believe that femininity is taking responsibility for our
bodies, so that the body becomes the tangible expression of the
spirit within. For those of us who have lived life in the head,
this is a long, difficult and agonizing process, because in
attempting to release our muscles, we also release the pent-up
fear and rage and grief that has been buried there, probably
since or before birth. Within ourselves we find a stricken animal
almost dead from starvation and mistreatment. Because it has
been punished so long, it acts at first like a wild neurotic creature
that hasn't known love. But gradually it becomes our friend,
and because it understands the instincts better than we, it
becomes our guide to a natural, spiritual way of life.

Marion Woodman[2]

* * *

They had travelled so far. The paths had been steep and treacher-
ous. Now she felt the first stirrings in her body. Her womb began
to tighten like a fist, gathering all her energy into its center, ready
to explode outward like a dying star. She was exhausted and
covered in dust. There were noises and commotion everywhere.
Bodies jostled and pushed past them, oblivious to the presence
pulsing within her. Her eyes implored the man standing with
her.

He stared at her, a jolt of recognition charging through his body
like electricity. The time had come. All the preparations, all the

plans, all the secret promises they had made together vanished. How could he protect her? He had only his arms and the love in his heart. Quickly he led her away from the crowds. The natural protection of rocks and grasses must make for her a home. The warmth of the earth and those breathing creatures could offer her a lair.

She walked slowly, stopping every few minutes to honor the flowing waves of pain shooting sparks through her. Her eyes never left his face, filled with a depth and a neediness which kept him transfixed on her. He allowed himself to be drawn into her depth, connected to her by invisible threads, at one with her painful opening.

Without taking his eyes from her face, he gathered sticks and made a simple fire. Rainwater was trapped in a small pool nearby and he set some to boil over the crackling flames. The range of the fire threw gentle shadows on the earth, the huge body of a woman in her fullness, moving in and out in a rhythm as old as time. The shadows from the rounded haunches of the animals were comforting, solid and strong, and the mist from their breathing gave warmth and life to the place.

She moaned softly, lost now in her own world. The animals watched, munching contentedly, unperturbed by this most ancient of miracles. A larger shadow was thrown over the woman as the man bent forward to encircle her, rocking her gently in his arms in motion with the sway of her rippling belly. She rose to her knees, head thrown back, her face shining in the moonlight. Never will I forget this moment he thought, as he looked at her glowing skin. Suddenly he saw the black hair protruding from inside her body. He reached gingerly to touch it, and then brought the woman's fingers to caress its bloody dampness. He could feel the joy flow through her and give her new strength. He prayed silently for the grace and knowledge his calloused hands would need to guide this child into light.

He watched in awe as her body blossomed outwards. His hands rested lightly beneath the tiny head as it slid from its dark passage. Now the shoulders emerged one by one. There he was, small enough to lie in the man's hand — a screaming, writhing human being, covered with the blood and water of his own long journey. The man offered him to the woman tenderly. She cradled him against her body, and the tiny limbs visually softened and melted back into her skin. The man carefully whispered encouragement to the woman as she pushed the bloody food of her body out onto the straw. Reverently he gathered it up and buried it deep in the earth nearby, a fertile gift of thanks for earth's shelter.

He fetched the warm rainwater and torn rags, and cleansed the child's body, and then the woman's. He prepared a fresh bed for them, and settled them together to rest. Through her tears, the woman smiled her thanks. No one but you, her eyes told him. Joy filled the air. Whatever was to come this time was theirs. Through, with, and in them love was now incarnate. Everything was possible.

* * *

The way of the mother began with the birth of my daughter, Rebecca. During the months of pregnancy, I worked hard, planning and preparing to give birth. My husband, Albert, and I attended classes where we breathed in unison, learned to relax and talked about decisions we might have to make during labor and delivery. My doctor's visits were rushed and impersonal. Questions were answered routinely as if they held little significance. By implication, the suggestion for the best course of action was to leave everything to him.

One hot Sunday, days after my scheduled date of delivery, Albert whispered to me that he was sure the baby was coming. The day felt magical and serene and we went to bed that night full of expectation. At midnight the ancient signs began. We began to time the contractions, looking at each other in wonder and fear, trying to rest as we had been advised to do. As the contractions came more quickly, we decided to head for the hospital which was close by.

We walked down the three flights of stairs slowly and out into the silence of the night. The moon was high in the sky, round and friendly. It made a good spot to focus on as the rippling pain flowed over my belly. It was 3 a.m. The street was completely deserted. My husband stared at the moon, his arm supporting me firmly as I leaned half on him and half on a lamppost. My knees were very wobbly. Later he would write in a poem: "with aves of the moon cooling the anxious earth"[3] to describe that

moment. Our first child was coming. He smiled, encouraging me
to walk on toward the hospital.

The hospital interior was quiet and sterile. They gave me a bed
with white curtains around it and a blue and white johnny which
clearly didn't fit! In the bed next to me, an unknown young
woman screamed and wailed. She was alone. At some point
during the night they sent her home. The pain increased. Albert
stayed with me, occasionally dozing in a plastic brown chair next
to my bed. I could feel his sense of impotence as he fumbled to
comfort me with a small white washcloth the nurse handed him.
The hospital bed made it difficult for us to sit close together and
walking around seemed impossible. We spent a long night vigil
whispering and breathing together, surrounded by strange smells
and eerie sounds. Occasionally a nurse joined us to check my
cervix, put instruments on my belly and offer a few encouraging
words. I felt proud of my control over the pain.

At nine thirty the next morning the all clear was given to begin
pushing. Straining and sweating, my body bore down again and
again, pushing the baby into the world. Albert yelled jubilantly
from the foot of the bed. He could see the head. With each
contraction a patch of wet black hair appeared, then retreated
inside me. Albert's face grew worried as he watched the baby
emerge and slip back again and again. He rubbed my back, held
my legs, sat behind me, but all to no avail. The doctor began to
make his rounds. As the minutes and hours passed, I began to
dread the sight of his snakeskin shoes approaching under the
curtain. His question was always the same. Was I ready yet to go
to the delivery room so that he could birth the baby? Each time I
gritted my teeth and said no. He wanted to play golf he joked.
When was I going to be sensible and admit defeat.

Four hours later the instrument on my belly registered a dis-
tressed heartbeat. My exhaustion was total. Calmly I let them take
me into the delivery room amid frantic professionalism. People
rushed around me, organizing instruments and explaining proce-
dures. It was a crisis. The delivery room was horrible, with cold
steel and bright lights all around me. I braced myself, numbing
my emotions as the anaesthetic numbed my body. Albert seemed
far away. He watched as a stranger cut me with a scalpel within
an inch of our baby's head, and pulled her out of my body with
forceps. A piercing cry rang out as she flew gracefully through

the air. Minutes later, our daughter lay on my chest, sleeping peacefully. Her tiny round face was rosy red. Fear and anguish evaporated into joy and gratitude. I thanked everyone profusely. The doctor paternally patted my shoulder offering his congratulations. He assured me that I had done everything possible to have a natural birth.

Later, I lay in another hospital bed alone. My new daughter was in the nursery and the anaesthesia was receding. I vaguely wondered why I felt so cheated.

Six months later, Albert wrote a poem about Becky's birth. His poetry captures the birth's inner reality regardless of the outer circumstances:

CAROL AT REBECCA'S BIRTH

What night is this, the rose of your pubis,
Parting lips of the infinite, pouting
Outward like a kiss, opening like the
Wound of Jesus, spilling His water, His
Blood, the uterine wine of our salvation,
The word of peace in our flat and frightened world.
What night is this with
Sounds as strange as death,
With smells common as
Creation, the sounds
And smells of mammals?
Carol my woman
I love your milk,
I love your sweat.
Carol I love your blood
Your spit and your tears.
What night is this...this sacrament of flesh
And blood surprising the dawn with this gift
Of bread from Eden: seven pounds of God
Flung forth in splendor, beginning heaven
This very hour? Oh my child, my child, for whom
So long ago I lit a candle in
The vast cathedral of my loneliness!
Carol, bleeding womb of the immortal...
Carol, my sister in an ecstacy
Of pain, breathe for us your eternal breath...
Breathe the breath of Godhead into time.

What night is this? The God of Abraham
Is leaping in my loins! What night is this?[4]

When we conceived our second child I was elated. There was a
birthing conference taking place nearby and I went and listened.
A woman spoke about her body and its ability to give birth
naturally. The love in her voice, as she described her own
birthings, was infectious. Home again, I began searching for a
midwife who attended home births. This time I wanted to give
birth — it was my right as a woman and I could not relinquish it
a second time. With apprehension Albert and I talked through
many things. What if the child died? What if we panicked?

The first time we visited our midwife we sat on her porch on
a sunny day, sipping lemonade and talking. She understood our
experience and our hope for a different kind of birth. She told us
the story of her births. The first three were in the hospital. She
explained the increasing emotional pain which finally drove her
to seek a home birth for her fourth daughter. For many years she
had worked as a nurse in the labor and delivery wards. Her
empathy for women seeking a different experience was obvious.
All my prenatal visits were at her home. I looked forward to them
and the sharing we did together. Over and over she told me that
she was there to support me in giving birth my way in my time.
This was an experience of a lifetime and her role was only to
facilitate the process.

There was always time for questions and feelings. Her reverence as the baby grew was the same feeling I had had with my
first baby and had never been able to share with my doctor. The
whole family awaited the birth of this baby. Becky was part of
the journey of preparing for a new sibling. She took my blood
pressure carefully, speaking reassuringly to me as she acted out
the role of nurse. Her face lit up as she listened to the baby's
heartbeat and felt the body moving. The visits were fun for her.
There were plenty of toys — but also, the sense that she was an
important member of the team.

I collected everything I would need at the house. There were
baby clothes and blankets for warming in the oven, towels cut
into cloths to massage my body, and frozen juices and soothing
herbal teas. Each day I stencilled a few more bears on the walls
and wondered if this baby would ever appear. The nursery was

almost ready. The wicker cradle was decorated and waiting. My last visit with the midwife left me in tears as we discussed natural ways to induce the baby and the tests needed if labor did not begin. Would this pregnancy last forever?

That same night, mysterious movements as old as the tides in the ocean, began to rock my body. It was night-time. I sat alone in the dark as the waves of pain intensified, praying for guidance and openness. My midwives arrived in the middle of a freezing January night. We made tea. Fear gripped me; the pain was powerful. Could I go through with it? I lost control. I clung to my husband and to the women. I was terrified that the process would stop like it had last time. I was terrified I wasn't doing it right, that I was too weepy, too scared, and too vulnerable. Yet it was delightful to just be myself, to be home. I took baths. I drank tea. The women reminded me that I could trust my body's timing, there was no hurry. Their encouragement and patience soothed me. We talked and laughed and whispered between contractions. There was a holy and hushed atmosphere in the house. A deep mystery was taking place and the air was charged with the significance of it. New life was coming.

The birthing was agony. I cried out. I thought I would be ripped in two. I was terribly needy, but I was allowed to be. It felt good to have people there whom I trusted. I needed them and I let myself need them. No one told me to be quiet, to pull myself together, to breathe correctly. As each contraction began, they nodded. They knew the pain. They also knew the value of it and kept affirming that. The connection between Albert and me deepened that night. My need of him was so primal that it was our birth and not mine. I could not have done it without him and his tenderness, and he knew it.

Becky woke at dawn in time to see the first hairs of the baby's head. She gave me courage. Her excitement was contagious. Through the haze of my concentration I could see her jumping up and down from foot to foot. Every so often she ran over and flung a wet cloth in my face, which was her task. It felt horrible, but it would bring me back to reality. The baby's head emerged. Albert stretched out his hands and received our child. He blessed her and gave her to me. I cried out "My baby, my baby" from the depths of me. I know because Becky remembers it. The tiny body lay against my skin. Once her breathing had settled, Albert cut the umbilical cord. I offered her my milk and she suckled gently. Time seemed to stand still and I have no memory of delivering the placenta, so enraptured was I with my new daughter.

Becky rocked her sister carefully, quietly absorbing her mixed feelings towards this tiny newcomer. A friend made breakfast, a meal of celebration which tasted wonderful. I took a bath with my new daughter and dressed her in a tiny nightgown. Albert and I settled down for sleep, our baby between us, in our own bed.

The experience was so gentle, that is my major memory. Kateri was welcomed into the world surrounded by love, enthusiasm and joy. There were no harsh lights or loud voices, no cold steel or plastic cloths. She was not ripped away from me to be measured or given shots. She was not handled by many different professionals who, for all their caring, are not really connected to the individual in their hands. At home, the baby is special because she is born into her own space. She comes into an environment that is waiting for her, the place where she will live and grow from the beginning. She is welcomed in a way that befits her coming — with awe and wonder and grace. She is not a problem to be checked, but a person to be celebrated. She is coming home.

Something happened with the birth of my second daughter: my femininity deepened. Whereas my first experience of birth was a rite of passage into motherhood, this birth was a rite of passage into my self as mother. My body gave birth, my body knows how to birth. My soul gave birth, my soul knows how to birth. That knowing is feminine wisdom; wisdom that is present within me. Many things block my access to that wisdom, that intuitive knowing. Somehow I knew that I needed to give birth this way. My birth and growth as a woman was intricately tied up in my giving birth my way and in my home. My being was reconnecting to the ancient power of birthing, and I knew that this birth encompassed many births, both physical and spiritual.

Being a birthing woman is powerful. There is an energy and an atmosphere around birth that is holy and radiant. The "earthiness" of the female body and the bloody connectedness of mother and child is indescribable in its beauty. I shall never forget the painful ecstasy of Katie's body emerging from mine into light. Carrying children and giving birth to them has allowed me to love and accept the sacredness of my body, and the life-giving strength and integrity of being a woman. It has allowed me to claim responsibility for my body and her wisdom, and to treasure my communion with all living beings who share in the experience of birth.

This wisdom comes not only from the human body, but from the body of the ultimate feminine symbol, the earth. Experiencing Katie's connection to my body, gives me an experience of my connection to the body of the earth. I am an event of the earth, just as Becky is an event of my body. I am a child of her womb. I am dependent on her womb to provide good air to breathe, good water to drink, and good soil to grow food. Living in my head allows me to stop listening to the wisdom of the body and to forget this knowing. Enthralled with human intellect, it is easy to ignore my dependence and vulnerability. Valuing myself as a life-giver helps me to embrace my mother — the woman who gave me birth; my grandmother — the woman who gave birth to my mother; and the generations of women before me. Their lives were birthed from one source. They shared the same home — the earth.

The threats the earth faces, the constant devastation her body experiences, the poisoning of all that you and I need to nurture our bodies and our souls begins to become a personal issue. Pondering these things in my heart helps me to know that giving birth, being a mother, is a journey, a spiritual way. As I open to the way, it reveals secrets far deeper than I can imagine.

The way of the mother begins in the body. The body holds the key to the first step of the way and that key is found in birthing. By experiencing the longing to give birth, the body cries out for the seed of new life. In love that seed is planted and begins to take root. Gestation is the period of time when the growth and sustenance of the new life within takes place. This being within my being rivets my whole energy — physical, emotional, mental and spiritual. A mother's womb is the habitat for her child. Every activity of her body affects that habitat. Each thought and feeling and each food or drink she consumes either nourishes or starves the life within her womb. The greater the attention and energy that the mother focuses on her growing child, the greater the feeling of connectedness between them. The child feels her mother's attentiveness or lack of it, her expectation and dread, her fear and hope, and her love or indifference. The child shares completely in the physical, emotional, and spiritual environment of the mother.

When a woman is with child she is blossoming with life. In his love poem, "Every Day You Play," Pablo Neruda writes:

> Mis palabras llovieron sobre ti, acariciandote.
> Ame desde hace tiempo tu cuerpo de nacar soleado.
> Hasta te creo dueña del universo.
> Te traere de las montañas flores alegres, copihues,
> avellanas oscuras, y cestas silvestres de besos.
> Quiero hacer contigo
> lo que la primavera hace con los cerezos.

In translation it reads:

> My words rained over you, stroking you.
> A long time I have loved the sunned mother-of-pearl
> of your body.
> I go so far as to think you own the universe.
> I will bring you happy flowers from the mountains,
> bluebells,
> dark hazels, and rustic baskets of kisses.
> I want to do with you
> what spring does with the cherry trees.[5]

While we do not own the universe, we certainly participate in it. Our bodies are the earth. Our minds and hearts are the earth's chance to think and to love. The human is the only species in which the earth attains consciousness. Through the human, the earth can see her beauty; through the human the earth can hear the music of the wind; through the human the earth can reflect on matter and mystery. When a woman blossoms with child, evolution moves through her.

The desire in women for motherhood is as deep as the history of life on earth. It is a desire that is manifested not only physically, but on every level of existence. Women desire to mother spiritually, to birth new life from the flow of divine mystery. Women desire to mother emotionally, to birth new life for themselves and others through feeling. Women desire to mother thought, to birth creative ideas and visions from the depths of feminine wisdom.

As women, we can take responsibility for this desire. Women

can choose to give birth. As Mary Rosera Joyce says in her book
Women and Choice:

> Responsible choice is like a woman giving birth. I once talked by
> phone with a woman whose labor pains were beginning after a
> very difficult pregnancy. There was reason for her to be afraid. We
> talked about receptivity. Suddenly she had to leave, and we hung
> up. The next morning she called from her hospital bed and said
> her labor and delivery were short and easy, and that she kept on
> repeating to herself during that time the word "receive, receive"
> and practicing it. "It is such a beautiful word," she said. We deliver
> our own stages of life, and choose our own actions, often in labor
> pains. Receptivity can make the process quicker and easier.[6]

The process of birth begins with receptivity. We hollow out a
space in the heart, and prepare the soil for planting. We wait
with desire, with expectance. As we wait, we begin to know what
we want. We want new life. We want hearts that can conceive
the seed of wisdom. We want hearts that are radiant with that
wisdom, so that it flows out to others. We want to bring to birth
all that we are as women, because we know that it is through,
with, and in us that life evolves.

Some years ago there was a weekend workshop to encourage
people to open to their feelings about the future of life on earth.
Participants worked in small groups sharing their despair for the
world, gently letting go of their denial. As we felt our common
fear, helplessness, and grief for the violence and destruction of
life all around us, our hearts opened and connected. A safe place
was created to feel the pain of our world. Suddenly from the far
side of the room, a woman birthed a bloodcurdling scream and
began yelling, "I'm so angry...I'm so angry" as she beat her body
against a mountain of pillows. It was the cry of rage of a mother
who watches the life she loves and longs to protect squandered
and desecrated before her eyes. That cry lives on. That woman
took responsibility for birthing the cry of the earth which is in all
our hearts.

The new life that burst forth from that woman, bloody and
sore, opened many people at that workshop to their longing for
a passionate response to the earth. Once the earth's need becomes
present, a response becomes imperative. People long for answers
and a way through crisis. That woman's despair and rage was a

turning point. It empowered all of us to come together and labor to birth hope for the future. Each of us came to connect with our personal response, knowing that it is part of the whole. Without it, the whole will be diminished. Each thread in a tapestry is crucial. The strength of the finished product is in the integrity of each thread. As we reached out to each other to form community and to provide a place to share our despair and hope, we reinforced a vision. It is a vision rooted in history, drawing on the power of the life that has already unfolded and proved there has always been a new birth. That new birth has been provided by individuals, individuals willing to be pregnant with prophecy and change, individuals opening themselves to provide the soil for new life, individuals ready to be used.

This is the essential mystery of carrying new life. When a woman is pregnant, the baby in her womb uses her body. The child draws all that she needs from her mother. When I was with child, I could feel the pull of life from my body to Becky. My role was to give her life, and she was the primary recipient of all nourishment and energy. She took what she needed before my needs were met. I gave her a physical home and she lived from me. In receiving, she gave me a gift. My need to give, to over-flow, and to nurture was totally received. This same interaction takes place between the earth and the pregnant mother. The mother takes all that she needs from the earth and gives to the child in the womb. The earth gives life and I take from her before her needs are met. When I consciously receive from the earth, I give her a gift.

In reality, a woman with child is a vent for the earth and her newest unfolding of life. The evolution of life which has been unfolding for billions of years, now moves through a woman's body creating a totally new person, unique and absolutely neces-sary. What will she bring this little one? What fraction of meaning and beauty will she bring to life? What radiance will be hers? As a mother, I am used to form her. Without me she will not exist, creation will be robbed of her preciousness, and yet she will be free to move beyond and away from me. We are separate and distinct, intimate beyond telling, yet distant. Life uses me to bring forth new life.

Everything that happens to the body in the months of waiting, the hours of labor, and the awesome moments of birth happens throughout the journey of life. That woman's explosive rage burst forth with the same pressure that a baby's head pushes through the final gate of a woman's body. The process of birthing is all around us. Once the process is embraced, we can begin to be midwives to ourselves and to others in our journeys of gestation, labor, and birth.

This process of birthing is one of the primary dynamics of the cosmos. "Drawn into existence by allurement, giving birth, then drawing others into existence — this is the fundamental dynamism of the Cosmos," says physicist Brian Swimme.[7] The earth's history is a history of birthing. Each stage in evolution birthed new life. The earth herself is formed from the stardust of an exploding star. A star burns and burns until all the elements in its core are used up, growing in intensity as it reaches the final stages of its fullness — like a pregnant woman. Then, it simply explodes outward scattering its riches throughout the cosmos. From these dust clouds, matter is again attracted to itself beginning another period of gestation. A second generation of stars is born, galaxies are formed, and the small planet which is our home comes to birth. Earth goes through many periods of gestation, violent labor, and birth.

The 4.6 billion years of earth's history is the story of how life began, how the conditions were created over time for the emergence of living cells in the oceans, and how these began to replicate themselves and adapt. How from each successive generation new organisms and new life functions emerged. Eyes were developed and sight became a function of the cosmos. Life continually refined and improved on itself until mammals evolved. These creatures, our ancestors, birthed their young from their own bodies. Our way of birthing had entered the earth process.

As the earth births new adaptations and new species, she mysteriously remembers what works and what does not. She is able to improve and refine life's advances to higher states of complexity, while at the same time she allows species and adaptations which do not "fit" to perish. Thus within every cell in my body is coded the memory of all these "successes" that have been slowly tested over time. My body and psyche know what works, know how to birth new life, and know instinctively how to allow birth to take place.

We share an awesome history. Each of us is a function of billions of years of birth and death and rebirth which is the cosmic story. Without each groping stage in life's unfolding, you and I would not be here. Birth is intrinsic to each of us. As a woman I have the remarkable privilege of partaking in this ancient and life-giving process.

When the process of birth is fully embraced, what wisdom does it offer? What lessons does a birthing woman learn to carry with her into daily life and into the lives of others? In relating the stories of my daughters' births, it is clear that their different circumstances are not just external, but primarily internal. As my inner self changed, I was able to choose the kind of birth I wanted, to take more responsibility for the birthing process and my role in it.

What I learned about myself and the unfolding of life in the four years between my daughters' births has been confirmed and deepened. Giving birth is the way of the mother. The dynamic of birthing is the metaphor to embrace in every aspect of life and death. It is the way life evolves. If I live the process then I shall be part of the flow of life, rather than one more obstacle along the way — both to myself and to others.

Birth demands an attitude of trust, a surrender to the process. Once a woman's body contracts for the first time, a process has begun that will continue to unfold to completion. There is fear in this. Once labor begins, it cannot be stopped. Trust in the body's ability to give birth is crucial. Remembering our origins and our animal nature helps to alleviate the fear. Every cell of the female body knows about birth.

My family was lucky enough to watch our cat give birth. She chose a box of old clothes under Katie's crib for her labor. Katie noticed her there, and called me, sensing at two years old that something big was about to happen. We lay flat on our bellies next to the crib, watching quietly. There was no fuss. Ginger knew what to do and just stared at me during her birthing, her eyes deep and full. One of the kittens got stuck halfway out and I tried to help her, but she moved away and began walking in circles with the kitten hanging out until he slipped out naturally. How proud and satisfied she looked when her three kittens were all cleaned up and suckling gently. She was very young to be a mother and I was worried, but I need not have been. Her instincts took over, instincts that have been reinforced over millions of years. Those instincts can be reclaimed. I can surrender to birth's outcome and welcome the new life it brings. I can choose to trust life and its unfolding, believing that the thrust of life is ultimately to fuller life and radiance.

Birthing teaches women a willingness to suffer. An animal giving birth suffers gracefully. Graceful suffering is not easily embraced in our culture. Yet birth is physically painful. If there is denial of the suffering when the process becomes painful, it is fought with gritted teeth, which only causes greater discomfort and fear. Relaxing, choosing the pain, and imaging the body as a flower opening with each contraction is gentler for both the mother and the baby. She feels and experiences her labor instead of running from it. There is ecstasy in choosing to feel pain. It loses its ability to control and, instead of the enemy, becomes a cherished ally in the task at hand. The joy and the ecstasy of birthing are more profound because of the pain, not in spite of it. Life, and all growth, involves suffering. When suffering is welcomed as one of life's seasons, it deepens and enriches the soul. It teaches endurance and strength. When pain is befriended, it carves out a space within and enhances self-respect. When I flee pain, believing it to be unnecessary or cruel, or I meet it with self-pity or helplessness, I fail to receive its gift. Birth teaches the value of suffering, for only the painful opening allows the new life to come forth.

Birthing is emptying. This is true not only physically, but also emotionally. In birth everything falls away except the process. Ideas and images of how things should go or be dissipate. The process cannot be controlled, it can only be allowed to happen. Emptying ourselves requires accepting ourselves as we are, not as we wish to be. It brings us to a state of humility.

Birth's greatest wisdom is the teaching of vulnerability. Trusting, embracing pain and emptying the self are all ways of becoming truly vulnerable. The key difference for me in my second physical birth was that I allowed myself to be needy. I received my husband's love and support. I relied on the presence of the women. I let myself be weak and scared. When I take this vulnerability into my life, I risk my true self. The physical act of birthing exposes a woman in her deepest vulnerability. The opening of the cervix and vagina resonates with the spiritual and emotional opening of the heart. This is why it is so important for birthing women to feel safe and to be in a nurturing environment. That depth of openness simply cannot be entered into otherwise.

We need that openness in all our birthings. Often in the process of birthing a new level of awareness, a person may experience great anxiety. It is important that there be an understanding friend or guide to act as midwife so that he may open up and enter his vulnerability. Risking vulnerability opens us to God's power and strength. Experiencing our inner weakness and fragility allows us to feel God's love, and the strength that comes from the knowledge of that love. It is a strength that births compassion, because it embraces pain as a way to come closer to God.

Moments of birthing are often preceded by periods of pain, panic, chaos, and vulnerability. All birth has its time of labor. If the wisdom of birth is intuitively grasped, the process can be accepted more calmly. Invariably, it is in those last painful pushes of the birthing process when we think we can take no more, that the new life mysteriously breaks through.

Surely, the most important thing to remember about the process of birth and the willingness to be a mother, is that without it God cannot be born. The power of God can only be birthed through, with, and in you and me. God needs us to be mothers; God is always waiting to be born. All of us, men and women, can only say "Yes" to giving birth if we know how to embrace the process of birthing and allow it to happen. Giving birth is about accepting our responsibility for bringing new life into the world in every sense. It is a task that we cannot give over to others. There is no one "out there" who will birth our life. It is through each unique life that the future can evolve; through faith, love, and hope as they are reflected in relationships, in lifestyle, and in community. As I learn to surrender more deeply to the love of God, I become a chalice for new life. New life is needed on every level of our human existence. Each of us contains a spark of divine life which we can birth for the whole. That birthing will enrich our lives and the lives of others. Life, itself, will be enriched and birthed anew.

As a woman, I feel allured to birth a way of the mother. I enter into the mystery of who I am and allow that to be birthed. Women everywhere are participating in the great work of birthing a feminine consciousness. I believe it is the work of the earth, for the earth knows that if we do not do it, she will perish. The discovery of the feminine will reconnect us to the ground of our being, the earth. I fear that if we do not birth this wisdom, this feminine way of being, we shall destroy not only ourselves as a species, but the earth herself.

Our lifestyles are so toxic to the earth's systems that there are serious questions among scientists as to when the earth will simply stop birthing life. The diversity and variety of the waste products that our technology continues to pour into the earth systems of the soil, the air, and the water are dangerously overriding the earth's ability to birth. In the same way that overtechnologizing the birth process has increased the interference in the natural way of birthing our children, so has our technology on the larger scale interfered with the earth's ability to birth life. The return to natural and simple ways of birthing children empowers us as women and connects us to the needs the earth has as a birthing mother.

I am still giving birth in so many ways. It is the same process as the birthing of my daughters — painful, joyful, and uncontrollable. A process that once begun cannot be stopped, although, like physical birth, it can be interfered with. It is my wounded heart that is giving birth, slowly opening as my body opened so that it can bleed freely and I can feel the mystery of God's new life. Daily I try to risk vulnerability, to surrender to the pain and to honor and welcome the child that comes forth. It is the divine feminine, wisdom's child that is growing within me waiting to be born. To birth her I need to find the way of the mother. I begin by honoring my rite of passage into motherhood by giving birth in freedom and in dignity.

CHAPTER TWO

Beauty
The Revelation of Love

What Beauty discovers, symbolic of the feminine spiritual center, is that her real beauty is her courageous vulnerability, her readiness to be open to the mystery of the unknown.

Linda Schierse Leonard[1]

She walked slowly, her eyes trying to take in the beauty of the place. The stone stairs she climbed had been worn smooth by many feet, their searching steps leaving a hollow well in the center of each slab. Her feet slipped into each space with ease, and she pondered the thought that even the most solid of matter softens in time with touch. She raised her eyes quickly. The size of the place filled her with awe. It was almost threatening. Huge arches and walls rose skyward on every side, making her a tiny figure moving hesitantly through their majesty.

She pulled the small bundle she carried closer to her body, and smelled the warm fragrance in the air. This was a place outside of time, an ancient holy place, full of silence and mystery. She tiptoed softly, lest her footsteps announce their coming. The man walked a little behind her, his wooden stick making a muffled sound as it rhythmically tapped each stair. She glanced at him, his body straight and tall, his head slightly bowed. Her eyes smiled her love and his mouth softened to a quick smile. He nodded her onward.

A small sigh escaped from the woven blanket in her arms. She pulled back the blanket's corner, and cooed softly to the sleepy face inside. His eyes opened wide and his little body stiffened into alertness as he caught the strange sights and smells. She smiled down at him, her heart pierced anew by the beauty of her child. He missed nothing, his eyes and ears absorbed every new moment with wonder and delight. What to her might be commonplace, was for him a thing of sheer beauty. The smell of her breast made his body squirm, and the love in his eyes as he suckled, staring at her face was almost overwhelming. His hand would reach toward her cheek, flailing to touch his most precious gift in all the world.

Up she walked, her step lighter and more confident. Why be afraid, when within her heart and arms were all she needed of the beauty which now surrounded her. Whatever was built by human hands to signify truth and glory was being built now within her soul. She bowed her head and kissed his soft hair, full of gratitude for her life. She knew she must bring him here to this holy place and offer him as a gift. She could do so, knowing too, that there was time yet for him to dwell close to the temple of her body, protected for a while by the seamless garment of her love.

*   *   *

The South Bronx paints a perfect picture of abandonment. There are empty buildings, lots piled with old tires and furniture, graffiti on every wall. In the midst of the desolation is an old Polish church, once also abandoned, now the home of a small group of Franciscan friars. Vowed to a life of poverty, they run a shelter for homeless men, and share themselves with their neighbors — people dying of AIDS who have left families behind, people begging, borrowing and stealing to satisfy their crack habits; people for whom muggings and shootings are part of daily life; children who come to the door regularly to eat, to talk, to help out, to play basketball.

On this grey winter day, the old Church is packed with people; many kinds of people. People from wealthy New York suburbs sit alongside people without homes. They are joined together to witness the ordination to the priesthood of a man who has waited many years for this moment. He is lying face down on the stone floor, his arms flung wide, his body prostrate in surrender. Angel voices chant the litany of saints. His mother, seated next to him, weeps, gazing at his strong body with visible love, watching her only son give himself forever to a life of poverty.

The first Mass is about to begin. Muffled laughter fills the Church as the new priest paces nervously behind the altar. The procession of priests and brothers makes its way to the altar. The ritual begins. The smell of incense filters through the air. Words ring out "Comfort, give comfort to my people"..."Like a shepherd he feeds his flock"...."Make ready the way of the Lord, clear him a straight path." The celebration unfolds, building momentum to the moment of sacrifice.

He stands, in homespun cloth, a slight figure with blazing eyes, holding the white bread high over a black plate. The community is silent. "Take, eat, this is my Body." Familiar words capture new meaning as he speaks them for the first time. A shepherd now, it is time to feed his flock. He steps forward cradling the consecrated bread and stands ready to offer to those he loves the ripened food of his longing. As he holds the holy food out to his mother, to his father, he weeps silently. One by one relatives and friends process towards him to receive the gift of nourishment, a seed of love grown within the fruit of sacrifice. His tears continue to flow unchecked and he lets them be. Many weep with him. Hearts are opened, their captives set free. My daughter, Becky, cries beside me. Laughing through her tears, she whispers, "I don't even know why I'm crying, Mummy." Moments of beauty exist for which there is no explanation.

Beauty sets our hearts free. Beauty causes our beings to tingle, and draws us out of ourselves and expands who we are. Beauty pierces us with a sweet mixture of pain and joy. Beauty connects us to life and to others, to mystery. Beauty gives us moments of heightened awareness and love.

Beauty calls out to us. Beauty invites us to interaction through our senses. Brian Swimme calls this interaction allurement. Our journey as human beings is to respond to allurement in our lives. If the beauty of Chopin's music allures me, I allow my sense of hearing to take me deeper into the world of his sounds. If I am allured by the beauty of freshly baked bread, I allow my sense of smell to open more deeply to the mystery of baking, or persuade my husband to make it more often. If my heart opens at the sight of a work of art, I allow my sense of sight and my imagination free rein and respond to the interaction between my being and the shapes, colors and spirit of the work.

When I was a child, there were long brown velvet curtains in the living room of our home. They were new and expensive and I was not allowed to play with them. I remember creeping into the room to touch them one day. Their rich texture made my fingers tingle, the sensation leaping from nerve to nerve throughout my body. It was an unpleasant feeling, in a way, like hearing a fingernail scratching a blackboard, but it was also irresistible. The sheer beauty of the cloth and the powerful response of my body drew me back again and again. When I was in my twenties, my father gave me a small velvet shoulder bag. The front flap is a scene depicting a house with a front path leading to the door, surrounded by fields. The embroidery on it is beautiful, and the colors and textures are vibrant and varied, some silk, some cotton, but mostly velvet. It is my favorite bag, and I still find myself stroking the flap and feeling again the beauty of the interaction between my skin and the velvet.

Beauty is truly in the eye of the beholder. Annie, a rag doll, is a member of our family. She has been with us for years — her red hair is almost gone — her clothes have been lost. Her black eyes and red nose have been replaced and worn away many times — her legs and arms and body parts have all been patched. She still looks tattered despite all the care and love lavished on her. At one time she went everywhere with us and Albert and I spent more time than we care to remember returning to stores, peering under cars in parking lots, retracing our steps, in efforts to find a lost doll. In the beginning, like the Velveteen Rabbit, she was splendid. Sitting in the corner of the crib, when my daughter was first born, she looked stunning. As an infant, Becky somehow learned to pull on her apron so that Annie flopped forwards and lay across her face. Once, worried that she might suffocate, I took Annie out of the crib. A sleepless night ensued. Annie had her place.

Today, she is a real rag doll, falling apart at the seams. She does not go out much anymore, but she still has her place. Every night she sleeps with Becky, still held snugly against her face. One night when I was putting her to bed, she held her love up to me, her face glowing with pride, "Isn't Annie beautiful, Mummy?" she smiled. "Yes," I whispered, "she is full of beauty." As John Keats so rightly said, "A thing of beauty is a joy forever. Its loveliness increases. It will never pass into nothingness."[2]

What Annie is for one daughter, rocks are for the other. Rocks of every description are beautiful and precious. When we go anywhere some are carefully chosen to bring home. Watching soccer one morning, my daughter spent several hours filling a large container with muddy stones. I objected to carrying it home with all the rocks in it. I tried to reason with her to choose some and leave the rest. She stared at me defiantly as only a three-year-old can. How could she relinquish any of her treasures? Each one was different. I insisted. She refused stubbornly. I told her she must carry them. The container was heavy, but she somehow dragged and balanced it all the way to the car. As I picked it up and put it in, she smiled triumphantly at me. Our rock collection continues to expand.

How do we lose that childhood vision, when we can really sense the beauty in rocks and rag dolls? Katie is in touch with the fact that the earth births beauty, as she births all life. To her its obvious, as she explores every rock, tree and plant. The human is the first species to reflect on beauty. Never before has anyone been able to see, hear, taste, touch or smell the earth's beauty and consciously appreciate it. The question for our times seems to be whether the human can bear the experience of so much beauty, or as Swimme puts it "can the cosmos survive the vision of its own beauty?"[3] Children can accept it, but as we grow up and become consumed by all the responsibilities of life, perhaps it is too much and we have to cover it over, to sentimentalize it and ultimately to destroy it. If we can discover the child's vision, we can choose to simply stare in awe at the jewel which is our earth, to recognize the value of her beauty, and to treat her as we would any precious treasure.

To live this way is not easy. Receiving beauty is difficult. Beauty can only flow into open hearts. My awareness of this is most poignant in my relationship with my daughters. To appreciate their beauty I need to slow down, and so often my life is too hectic to respond to my daughters' needs in the moment.

When they sense that I am distracted, their demands for my attention increase. Implicit in their behavior is the agonizing plea for relationship, the need to connect with me, to be with me without "doing" anything. They want to gaze at my beauty, to love me, to contemplate me. I can tolerate that much love and beauty flowing from an infant, most of the time, but as my daughters grow and express themselves so openly, it becomes more painful to receive the beauty of those moments. There are days when an adoring gaze is like an arrow in my heart, piercing my own feelings of unworthiness. There is a wrench in my gut when my daughter pours out her love like a fire as she pats my cheeks over and over hardly able to contain her delight.

When I am in touch with my inner beauty, I see it clearly in my children and in the flow of love between us and I can receive their love into my heart, bask in it and let it flow back to them. I do not remember moments like these in my own childhood. When my daughters love me this way it awakens the needs I had as a child to show forth my beauty and to be received. Many of those needs were not met and feeling them is painful. Trying to give my daughters what I did not receive is frightening. I tend to close my heart, and thus block the beauty of their love.

If instead, I feel the pain, I can use the moments of my daughters' love as an invitation to grow, to uncover my wounded inner child and her beauty. If I refuse the allurement of their beauty, the call to deepen, I refuse their love for me and ultimately destroy their love for themselves. My daughters see themselves in the same way that I see myself inside, regardless of what I say. If I am unable to see myself as possessing beauty, they are unable to recognize it in themselves. To avoid the painful feelings, I have to handle their spontaneous affection for me by "civilizing" them. I subtly teach them to tone down their beauty, to control it and ultimately to let it die, the way I was taught. We "do things together" and fill our lives with activities. I crush the best part of them, their totally unselfconscious ability to love, to delight, to wonder and to be beauty. I prepare the soil for their emptiness to grow, their isolation and lack of connection to beauty. Thus they fit into a culture that will offer them a thousand and one ways to fill that empty place, each one as unsatisfying and addicting as the last. My children's inner rage at their loss of beauty will be the fuel that drives them to spend the rest of their lives building an external reality to prove that they really do have worth, that they are beautiful.

This same dynamic is present in our species' relationship to the earth. As people we have lost our connection to the earth and failed to value her beauty. Our deepest need is to be with the earth as mother, to touch her, to gaze at her beauty, to contemplate her features, to feel her body. Most of us can identify with the healing we experience after being close to nature. I know there are times when my body needs to be by the sea. I grew up near the ocean, and I need to return again and again to the healing rhythms of the tides. When we recognize and revere the earth's beauty she mirrors back to us our beauty as her creatures.

Modern lifestyles make it almost impossible to meet our need for natural beauty. Instead we compensate ourselves with "things," demanding more and more from the earth's resources and destroying more and more natural beauty to meet our demands. Scientific reports tell us that the earth is dying, that there are holes in the ozone layer, that all her life systems are poisoned and are shutting down. Yet we do not seem to hear, we do not seem to see the earth, to feel her, to mature beyond a relationship of using her. The inner rage at our loss of beauty drives us to build an external reality to mirror our worth back to us. But the reality we build by our consumption does not contain the love which true beauty reveals. An interaction, an allurement is necessary, and hearts hardened by possessiveness and fear are unable to risk the receptivity which would enable them to respond to the call. The experience of beauty is rapidly becoming absent from our lives.

Pondering the heart, slowing down, is a way of rediscovering beauty both within and without. It is a way of opening to allurement. One day I bought pansies to plant in my garden. In my hands were some of the earth's most beautiful riches. I experienced a deep satisfaction seeing their bobbing faces poking up from the soil. Each flower was different. Each one's color, smell, texture, and shape was completely unique. Pansies are just one breed. There must be millions of flowering plants, trees and shrubs. I eat their fruit daily without a thought. As I dug holes in the brown soil, I imagined an earth without flowers; a spring without snowdrops or crocuses; a fall without apples. The earth was 4,200 million years old before she brought forth her flowering riches. For all those years before her fruitful adolescence, she was barren of their splendor. There was a time when there were no flowers.

Holding the glowing purple petals of the final pansy to be planted, I imagined that this was the last flower the earth would grow. I allowed it to allure me with its beauty. What of its history and pre-history? For billions of years the earth labored to prepare the soil in which it grows. This flower is a member of a plant species that may have been living on the earth for hundreds of generations. This flower has roots in the soil and draws water and nutrients directly from the earth. It feeds on the sunlight absorbed by its leaves. Through the miracle of photosynthesis, it breathes in carbon dioxide and breathes out oxygen. It began as a seed. The seed broke open and died so that roots and a stem could spring forth. In interaction with soil, water and sunlight it grows, pursuing its journey towards light, giving itself to its task of providing beauty and fruit. This flower will live in my garden, producing fresh seeds, then dying, returning its body to the soil as food. It will be part of a living community. It knows how to live in harmony with earthworms and bees, cooperating in the cycle of giving and receiving, which is the dance of life.

A flower can be picked. Each stamen can be counted. The way in which it takes in moisture as food, and releases it as waste can be documented. A flower can be cut open and examined. It can be classified using a long Latin name. The analysis is thorough and accurate. The facts about this type of flower are printed in a book. I remember drawing the parts of a flower in biology class, how difficult it was, and how much I enjoyed the challenge of recreating the flower with paper and pencil. The danger is that because the flower can be dissected and drawn, because it can be named and all its parts analyzed by function, I could leave my biology class believing I know what the flower is, that I've seen it. I have information about it which I understand. I can explain to you everything about this type of flower. Yet if I only see it removed from the garden, its beauty is destroyed because the truth of the flower's interrelationship with its environment is missing.

Until a flower is seen in its living context, with an appreciation for its history, community and its task, the flower's full beauty is veiled. The significance and value of the plant and its mystery is lost. Knowledge can ignore beauty and mystery. The life of the flower cannot be explained or analyzed. It can only be experienced in gratitude.

In his reflections on the life of St. Clare of Assisi, Murray Bodo includes the following meditation on roses:

> Roses especially reminded her of who she was and of what she must become. They were so tight in the beginning, and then slowly, imperceptibly they opened up and surrendered themselves

to whatever lay about them. Even in dying they dropped their petals gracefully; and if you listened quietly enough, you could hear the silence of their falling. All that was left was the center, naked and free of all the pampering satin petals it held so closely at the start. And the center held in perfect poverty.[4]

Flowers can bring the heart to many places of beauty. The earth provides us with millions of varieties of flowering plants, shrubs and trees. When I touch or smell a flower, or share one as a gift of love, I try to revere the beauty and the relationship it has to the earth, to me, and the interconnectedness of the beauty among us. As I begin to allow myself to open to the call of beauty and become willing to follow that lead, life takes on new meaning. I enter a process of learning how to "see," how to be open to mystery, and my life becomes full of beauty once more.

As a young woman I embraced the cultural ideal of who I had to be. Beauty meant looking good on the outside and was achieved by using cosmetics, clothing tricks and sheer will power to whip my body into shape. My body was an object by which I was to be judged. All I ever saw was what was wrong with it, what needed to be covered up, disguised and eliminated. I was no longer living in my body but rather from a mental vantage point outside of it, struggling to have it reflect whom I thought others wanted me to be. I felt alienated.

The feminine body is beautiful. Her beauty is not the artifical celluloid beauty of the magazines, flawless and perfect, nor does it conform to a standard. It is said that Carl Jung described himself, near the end of his life, as "a little clod of earth." Our bodies literally are clods of earth, each different from the other. I had to decide whether I wished to continue to "develop" my clod into something artificial, or simply to be within it, celebrating and affirming my body's earthiness and allowing my body/self to show forth her own natural beauty.

What the culture does to the female body, it does to the earth. We paint over her natural beauty, strip her rich soil, tear down her vegetation and then rebuild her in our image, covering her with buildings, highways and malls. We then attempt to recreate her natural beauty by landscaping, creating parks and tastefully applying cultivated vegetation. Places like Disney World are examples of this kind of human re-creation of natural beauty. Make it more fun, more exciting, more titillating and generally more unrealistic. Why do we not encourage our children to wonder at the beauty of the night sky instead of taking them to Disneyland? Our need for real beauty is never deeply satisfied.

My first pregnancy allowed me to begin to be at home with the earthiness of my body. I had stopped wearing makeup about a year before as a first step in befriending my physical self. As I carried my first child, I felt extraordinarily beautiful. I watched my body swell and flower, displaying the miracle of my stretching skin and the rich heaviness of my body. As summer came I felt myself ripening, as my body prepared for its season of harvest. Then there was the milk, warm and sweet. The abundance the body offers its new life is the same as the abundance the earth offers us. Life is profuse, extravagant in the extreme. I knew the aching of the full breast, sore with its fruit, the sticky mess of overflowing milk. I needed to teach myself to value the hours I sat staring at the beauty of a baby's face, listening to the luxurious sound of enthusiastic suckling. It is hard to just be and behold beauty and know that it is valuable. So much of my experience pushes me to do, to keep busy, to achieve, to get things done.

We use no artificial contraception in our marriage. We chose a method of natural family planning and began to chart my mucus presence daily, learning how to "see" my fertility by observing the changes in the mucus pattern. I began this discipline with a sense of frustration at one more chore I had to fit into my day, but gradually my awareness of my body's changes has become a deep source of wonder for me. What a sense of power and joy I have on those days when I know my body is open and ready to receive new life. My feelings too are in tune with my body's cycle and I now have a deeper understanding of myself and my relationship to the wholeness of my life as I move through my monthly rhythms. I sense that I am more creative when my body is fertile and ready to conceive, and I am aware now when my body bleeds with the waning of the moon and ovulates with its fullness. Being able to "see" that my body and my larger body, the earth/moon system, are one is a gift.

This discovery of love for the richness of my body not only connects me to the body of the earth, but also deeply enhances the intimacy between my husband and me. Celebrating our mutual fertility gives us both a sense of the mystery of our roles as co-creators with life. Our communication is deepened and fostered by a sense of joint responsibility for this awesome power. Opening to the possibility of new life becomes a joint venture and a mutual celebration. If together we cannot embrace the total responsibility of a new being in our lives, we choose not to enter into union. The good of our relationship, our family life, our community and our earth all enter into our choice. Our freedom to love each other is more real within limits.

The mucus my body produces when it is ready to receive the seed of new life is also amazing. I imagine that the places where life first burst forth on the planet were similar to this crystalline and viscous stuff which teems with promise, like the ruby richness of the womb's sloughing-off each month with its physical and emotional mourning. I have come to honor the wondrous workings of my body instead of trying to get rid of them or cover them up. Ellen Bass' poem "Tampons" calls to me of the same longing to value ourselves as women and to celebrate our bodies' rhythms and mysteries.

> Our blood will feed the depleted soils.
> Our blood will water the dry, tired surface of the earth.
> We will bleed. We will bleed. We will
> bleed until we bathe her in our blood and she turns
> slippery like a baby birthing.[5]

Beauty awaits us everywhere. All that is communicates its beauty to us. One day I was sitting outside in a rocking chair. I was knitting a sweater that had a complicated floral pattern using many colors and requiring all my concentration. A nearby tree danced in the breeze. I tried to ignore it but my attention became riveted on it. The silvery branches danced and swayed, gracefully giving themselves to the flow of the wind. Time passed. I couldn't shake the sense that the tree was performing for me. My neighbor appeared and I commented to him on what a magnificent tree grew in his yard. He said he was planning to cut it down. He wanted to make a garden and it gave too much shade. I was distraught and told him so, pointing out the tree's beauty. Perhaps he could trim some branches. Had the tree known its plight and communicated it to me? The universe is a living organism, each part related and interconnected to every other part and to the whole.

Learning to feel beauty reveals something else. Beauty exists in relationships. When I am in touch with my own beauty, I can feel the beauty around me, and when I can feel the beauty around me it reflects back to me my beauty. Recently, there was a local meeting. A woman next to me was talking and her daughter kept interrupting and squirming. I beckoned to her to come and sit on my knee. She came over, a bubbly mass of jet black curls, eyes shining, and settled herself against me. This child is adopted, her life history is full of terror and abuse. She grinned up at me and laid her curls against my chest, snuggling into position like a cat. There she stayed. I stared at her, slightly afraid to embrace the gift of beauty which she so generously offered. The meeting faded away as we looked at each other in recognition. Inside every person is a child like this one, trusting, loving, full of beauty. As with the flower I will not feel that beauty unless I am willing to approach you as the unfolding mystery that you are. I cannot limit you based on my knowledge of your behavior; I cannot fit you neatly into a category based on your appearance in the moment. Instead I open to the whole context of your life history, realizing that every connection to life you have experienced up to this moment will have shaped who you are. I cannot approach you with this reverence unless I have first given it to myself and seen who I am as that same mystery to be approached with wonder.

I half expected that child to shun affection because of her history. My fear of appearing foolish might have stopped me from reaching out to her and then I would have failed to receive the gift she had for me. To the extent that I pre-judge you, I fail to feel your true beauty. When I am open to what is truly there in the moment, as with the flower, not only do I receive your beauty, I also connect with my own. The beauty of the flower is a part of me — it tells me something about my life. The beauty of a child teaches me about trust. Her joy and her pain are also mine. My joy in who she is and my pain at what she has suffered reveal something of beauty to her. We are one.

This reality of connectedness is an emerging one in our consciousness. The feminine in women and men has always intuited this depth of relatedness. Science is now beginning to prove empirically that reality is far more concerned with interconnections than with separate parts. For centuries the human perfected a way of breaking down parts and analyzing them, and this has naturally led us to see ourselves as separate, isolated parts in a mechanistic universe. Thanks to the breakthroughs begun by Einstein, we can affirm for ourselves and others that the true source of power is not in the ability to control others and in invulnerability, but rather in openness to others and in connection to them, and to the earth. When I am willing to affirm your beauty and power, I can share your resources as well as my own for the task of healing our world. The person with the most power is the one who can most deeply allow life to flow through her to others.

The beauty of the body speaks this truth. Each nerve interacts with every other, and energy leaps from one neuron to the next. This movement of energy is called synergy, the pathway of energy through an organism. We need to develop this synergy with and in community. As Joanna Macy so beautifully puts it, we became "synapses in the mind of God."[6] Our task is to allow the loving energy of that Mind to ignite us into beauty so that we may ignite the beauty in others.

In one of the Gospel stories, we meet a beautiful woman. Perhaps her hopes of love died long ago. Her dreams lie imprisoned behind walls of pain and cynicism. People jeer and yell insults at her when she passes by. The sun shines as she makes her way to the village through the deserted countryside. Today there are strange sounds ahead. She climbs a sandy ridge and stares at the scene below. A large crowd has gathered. People are sitting on the ground, grouped around a man. He is speaking to them, pleading gently, his hands outstretched. She creeps forward and finds a smooth rock to sit on. A woman next to her moves away. Her mind screams at her to run, but her body refuses to move. She listens intently to the man's words.

In those imaginary moments, that woman's heart experienced the beauty of the man, Jesus, and she responded. However she actually met him, it is clear from the story that she fell in love. Imagine yourself falling in love as she did with a charismatic person, someone whose touch, whose words, whose very presence awakens in you a deep sense of beauty. Later you discover that this person is visiting the town where you live. He has been invited to a local house for dinner. It is the kind of place that you would never be invited, too grand and exclusive. Yet your heart longs to express to the one who has changed your life what his beauty has ignited in you.

Risking everything, you go to him, uninvited, and taking precious ointment, you annoint his feet. You stroke and caress his skin, easing the tiredness there, pouring your energy and your passion into him. With your touch, you try to communicate your gratitude for the beauty that has transformed your heart. You feel his pain. You sense that his beauty is often crushed. You feel the price he pays for his vulnerability and his vision. Your tears fall and you raise your face to his, revealing your willingness to share his burdens. Kneeling forward you loosen your hair and with it tenderly dry the feet you have annointed with your love and with your tears. Sorrow and shame for all the times you have abused yourself and failed to appreciate your beauty and the beauty of others is poured out with your love.

The dinner guests are in an uproar. Anger and insults are aimed at you. But their outrage cannot destroy the mystery that is taking place. You have touched this man and he has received your love, which affirms the beauty and goodness of who you are. Beauty has flowed through your body, your hands, your tears, your hair in a gift of love. His heart has totally received the gift. Your risk has opened both of you to the beauty of the divine love flowing within and between your hearts. That love brings gifts of healing, unity and wholeness to both of you. You have each become beauty for the other and ignited beauty in the other.

I believe that woman's gift changed Jesus. Perhaps her loving action became a source of deep nourishment. Perhaps her vision of him was the encouragement he desparately needed to continue to risk himself and his message. We know that he praised her publicly, promising that she would always be remembered for her great love. But perhaps the most powerful revelation of the effect her love had on him came later. Before his death, at their last gathering, Jesus wished to show his closest friends how much he loved them. He wished to give them a sign of how they were to love each other. He knelt before them, one by one, and washed their feet. The beauty of that woman's love ignited a beauty in him that will always be remembered.

There is a deeper significance in this story. The woman is a symbol of the feminine earth. The earth kneels at the feet of the human. She offers us all the rich beauty of her body and gives her precious ointments without reserve. Dabbling hot, tired feet in a cool stream after a day of walking is a blessing. Having someone pour ice cold water over your feet on a stiflingly hot day, as my daughters once did, is sublime. It allowed me to feel something of the gift that is shared in the Gospel story. Sadly, in our relationship with the earth, we behave like the guests at this banquet, shouting insults and wanting only to destroy her courageous, vulnerable beauty because it threatens us. We cannot receive it. Our task is to become people like Jesus, secure and loving enough to receive the earth's beauty with grace, to allow that beauty to ignite us into a deeper relationship with its source, and to discover in that "moment in and out of time" the call to become beauty.

There is a yearning in the human soul for beauty's touch. I need to feel beauty. Part of the learning is to feel the beauty of all life's seasons and to know that beauty flowers when I am brave enough to choose vulnerability. I must be open to others' visions of beauty when I am blind and trust them. I need to allow the beauty of all that I encounter each day to heal and to nurture my spirit. Every small movement of life is precious. As I grow in sensitivity to beauty, I am empowered to celebrate and to protect it. I am motivated to continue my inner journey with hope, to work harder to feel and heal the beauty of the earth. Beauty calls out to me of the unity of all things, the common divine life which shows forth in everything. Beauty returns me to my origins. It grounds me in the earth, the mother of all that is beautiful, and it awakens me to the Creator who willed Beauty into being.

In Morris West's beautiful book, *The Clowns of God*, there is a description of a mongoloid child who is part of a community chosen to renew life on earth.

I know what you are thinking. You need a sign. What better one could I give than to make this little one whole and new? I could do it; but I will not. I am the Lord and not a conjuror. I gave this mite a gift I denied to all of you — eternal innocence. To you she looks imperfect — but to me she is flawless, like the bud that dies unopened or the fledgling that falls from the nest to be devoured by the ants. She will never offend me, as all of you have done. She will never pervert or destroy the work of my Father's hands. She is necessary to you. She will evoke the kindness that will keep you human. Her infirmity will prompt you to gratitude for your own good fortune...More! She will remind you every day that I am who I am, that my ways are not yours, and that the smallest

dust mite whirled in darkest space does not fall out of my hand . . .
I have chosen you. You have not chosen me. This little one is my
sign to you. Treasure her![7]

It is good to ponder whether I can reveal my beauty, my vulnerability, as the woman in the Gospel was able to do. Refusing to
be limited by custom or others' discomfort, can I share my vision
of the beauty I feel in you as freely as she did? Perhaps more
challenging still is to ask whether I can receive another's beauty
as Jesus received hers. Am I worthy of that kind of nurturing and
passionate love? Can I choose not to defend myself against it?
Whoever that woman was, I celebrate her passion and her longing. Think about a world in which we dare to feel the beautiful
in ourselves, in others, in everything around us. Imagine that we
trust what we sense is true and are willing to risk our own unique
response to what we feel. Imagine that we no longer hide our
love and our joy and our pain, fearing that to give it would be to
diminish what little we have. Imagine that we open our hearts
and give forth the beauty that is there, trusting that to reveal it
is to let our vision of Beauty be a fire that glows with divine love,
sending sparks flying throughout the cosmos.

CHAPTER THREE

Terror
The Invitation of Love

How should we be able to forget those ancient myths that are at the beginning of all peoples, the myths about dragons that at the last moment turn into princesses; perhaps all the dragons of our lives are princesses who are only waiting to see us once beautiful and brave. Perhaps everything terrible is in its deepest being something helpless that wants help from us.[1]

Rainer Maria Rilke

Nor can society offer a Great Mother image to reach out to, a mother who could help her to bridge the gap between herself and her femininity. That archetype is not yet constellated. Without that maternal matrix she moves alone in the landscape of her own terror, shrinking from the chaos of a new life and paralyzed by dreams of the old.[2]

Marion Woodman

Gone. The word was like a death knell. How could he be gone? Where was he? Why? Why? Why? Panic filled her; a dark all-encompassing terror, a screaming "no" from the depths of her soul. Her child gone. The growing dread she had felt as they searched now crystallized into certainty. He was lost, separated from her, gone. Howling wind bit through her clothes, exposing the emptiness of her being. She pulled the woollen garment closer to her body, but there was no comfort.

It was her fault. It was his. Her eyes reproached the man beside her. She was filled with an overwhelming sense of failure. Where was the infant she had caressed, the laughing toddler who had helped her knead bread? The boy child whose eyes were filled with longing and whose questions would shock her with their wise simplicity? What had she done wrong? Why would he go away? Cruel voices taunted her on the inside. Her heart ached.

38

The man took her arm and began to lead her back the way they had come, hurrying her to the place they had last seen him. She was besieged with wild terrors. She envisioned her child lying dead on the side of the road. She saw him in her mind's eye carried away by some drunken group of merrymakers and pushed the image away. He was still so young, still a child at heart. How would he manage alone and lost in such a large city? She had not prepared him for real life, she had not planned, she had not told him of the realities of many peoples' lives. No tears would come. Only tiny droplets which clung to her clothing as she panted heavily in the wind, struggling to keep up with the man beside her.

She no longer knew where she was, everything looked unfamiliar and strange. She let herself be pulled along, her mind racing. Help me, she pleaded, dear God, help me.

At that moment, she felt the solid weight of a door open in front of her, and as she came to her senses and looked around to see where she was, she saw her child. He was explaining quietly and with great conviction some point he had been making to those around him. He was completely involved in what he was saying. Anger boiled inside her and she began to yell accusations at him. How could he do such a thing? How could he be so unconcerned about her suffering? Even as she heard the first of her words, she knew that the boy in front of her was no longer hers. He had moved away from her. His own life had begun, a life she could not share. The loving intimacy that she had known with him until now was changed. She must let him go, free him to give to others the love she had given him. She had always known this day would come.

The terror swamped her again. Every fibre in her being wanted to run to him, take him in her arms and hold him there safe and secure. Surely a mother can protect her own child? But she knew she could not go to him. He had chosen his time to move away from her and she must watch him go. Only in her heart could she clothe him still with her love. She could only stand and watch him walk the path she had lovingly prepared him for. Terror would be her companion in the years ahead, a terror from whose dark depths her love must be birthed again and again. Her son would return home with his parents, but he would no longer come to her for comfort or to ease his fears. His terrors could no longer be softened by her arms. He was a man now, and would walk, like his fathers before him, alone, his life surrendered to the holy terror of the love of God.

* * *

A young couple, recently married, moved into one of the small terraced houses that lined the street. The residential neighborhood was like any other, rows of brick houses on either side of the street with stone walls and hedges along the sidewalks. At regular intervals, black wrought-iron gates allowed glimpses of narrow paths, bordered by flowers, leading to ornate front doors. The house with the circular stained-glass window in the front hall became their home.

The town was pleasant, an attractive seaside resort on the southern coast of England. Each working day, the husband left early to travel by train to London. He held a position at a small firm in the city. The woman who waved goodbye to him at the door was young and pretty. Loneliness tugged at her. The town was unfamiliar and she missed working in London herself. The days were long as she kept house and sought ways to meet people. When it was confirmed shortly after Christmas that she was to become a mother, her spirits soared.

Her parents came to visit that Easter and stayed the weekend. On Monday afternoon before their return trip, the four of them sat comfortably in the small living room, drinking tea. Her father, in a sombre tone, asked her a question. Had she been ill lately? No, she replied, she felt fine. She'd had a rash for a few days recently, but it was nothing serious. Her father's expression tightened. He explained carefully, in his most professional medical tone, that the rash was German Measles, an illness that severely affected a child in utero. A pregnant woman who contracted measles risked having a blind, deaf or otherwise physically abnormal child. Heart problems might occur. The risks were great. Therefore, he had arranged for her to have an abortion up north. It's the best course of action, he finished deliberately, staring at his daughter.

The young woman was dumbfounded. She glanced helplessly at her husband, who seemed stunned into silence. Her father continued. A professional associate of his would take care of it.

The procedure was planned for Wednesday morning. She was to come home with them tonight and by Friday morning she'd be fit enough to travel to London and meet her husband after work. No need to worry, it would be simple and painless. She was young, she'd have other children.

The look on her father's face was all too familiar. Memories of the few times she had tried to reason with him flooded back. Her opinion was never valid. Inevitably, an outburst of rage followed, replete with violent accusations of why she didn't love him. Her mother gave her a cheerful smile — how nice to have you home for a few days. Words of protest evaporated before they reached her lips. Numbly, she cleared away the tea tray, walked upstairs and packed a small bag. An hour later, as if in a dream, she found herself riding north in the back of her parents' car.

Familiar scenes passed by the window. White-capped waves crashing against the shore, fields dotted with grazing sheep, docks bustling with fishing boats and passenger ferries. The colors of the countryside glowed in the setting sun. Landscapes that normally cheered her seemed grey and ugly. The constant chatter of her parents exhausted her. The journey seemed endless.

After a near sleepless night at her parents' house, the usual round of visiting began. Her mother led her on a frantic mission of seeing friends. Superficial high-pitched chatter battered her mind. The real reason for her visit home was, of course, never mentioned. There was no time to feel anything.

That same morning, her husband travelled alone to the city, his mind full of worry. Normally he enjoyed the train ride, absorbed in the daily paper. Today, he was totally preoccupied, biting his nails mercilessly as he pondered alternatives. By the time the train pulled into the London station, he had arrived at a decision.

He walked quickly to the dignified office building in the heart of the City. He took the stairs two at a time and marched straight to the Chairman's office. The Chairman intimidated him, but his knuckles rapped firmly on the door before he could change his mind. A gruff voice from within granted him entry. Taking a deep breath, he opened the door. The old man behind the large wooden desk raised his head from a stack of papers and waved him to a chair. Hesitantly, the young man explained his request. Could he be excused for an hour today to consult the firm's doctor. He outlined the situation. Surprisingly, the old man readily agreed, and picking up the telephone, arranged an appointment for him that morning.

An hour later, seated in front of the doctor's desk, he again explained his dilemma. The doctor was puzzled. The speed of the decision was troubling. He agreed that a second opinion should be sought. He could recommend a good specialist in the City. He called the man's office to make an immediate referral. An appointment was not available until Wednesday afternoon. The young man nodded his assent.

For the rest of the day his thoughts were scattered. He dreaded the call he must make to his wife. Should he intervene this way? Her father's reaction was unpredictable. By evening he telephoned his in-law's home and spoke with his wife. He outlined the day's events. Would she be willing to come to London on Wednesday? The relief in her voice was tangible. Yes, of course. Her father was with patients just now, but she would explain as soon as possible.

Her father was called out on a home visit that evening and returned late. Already in bed, she tossed and turned in the familiar dark of her bedroom. Her bag was packed. A quick iron over her dress in the morning, then catch the train to the City. Her mind rehearsed over and over the words of explanation to her father.

He came into the room the next morning as she stood at the ironing board. One look at his face told her that her mother had given him the news. He stood with hands on hips, demanding to know what in God's name she thought she was doing. Did she want to bear a handicapped child? The doctor who was to perform the abortion this morning was doing him a personal favor. How could he cancel at the last moment? How dare she humiliate him this way? His voice grew louder and louder. Her bag and coat sat ready in the hallway. The ironing board was between them, the door on her right. She began to back towards the door. As she ducked out of the room, a sickening crash filled the air. The iron fell at her feet leaving a dent in the wall inches from her body.

Without a word she ran and kept moving until her body was seated on the musty train headed for London. Crumpled against the shabby velvet cushions, alone in the carriage, the tears came.

The specialist's office on Harley Street was plain but comfortable. A nurse ushered them into a large, sunny room, where a man with greying temples rose to shake their hands. The young husband spelled out the situation briefly, as he studied the man behind the desk, searching for advice. The doctor was listening very attentively, and when it came time to give his opinion, he began to talk softly.

He tried to put the young couple at ease. Yes, he explained, there were medical complications associated with German Measles and the child in utero. He listed the facts carefully. In his experience, perhaps one third of children born to women who had this disease during the first trimester of pregnancy, were born with some form of handicap. The effects were potentially very serious.

Yet, he continued gently, there were other factors to consider. The termination of a pregnancy, especially the first, could cause different problems. A woman may suffer emotional scars which last a lifetime. While the risks were real, the chance of the baby being born without abnormalities was good.

An hour passed quickly as questions were asked and possible outcomes discussed. His presence was calming. For the first time in two days the couple felt a sense of well-being and peace.

On the train ride home that evening, they sat surrounded by business men in hats and pin-striped suits, whose faces were hidden behind their evening papers. The young woman and her husband whispered together. As the train pulled into the seaside station, the decision was made. They would continue the pregnancy.

The days and months following were bittersweet, filled with a mixture of poignant expectancy and sudden fear. Her father rejected her completely. Don't blame me, his voice rang in her head, you'll be responsible for raising an abnormal child. She pushed the thoughts away. A busy social life helped to pass the months of waiting. The local tennis club and volunteer duties in the community filled her days with activity.

One Autumn day, labor finally began. It was slow and difficult and the doctor ordered anaesthesia so he could deliver the child with forceps. When the young woman awoke, a nurse laid her new daughter in her arms. She felt pride, mixed with apprehension, as she peered at the tiny face. The eyes were open. Could she see? Did she hear? The little body appeared perfect. The rosebud mouth sought her nipple with enthusiasm. The mother smiled.

Six months later, after many noisy experiments with saucepan lids and flashing lights, medical checkups and observations, a crate of scotch whisky with a letter of thanks arrived at the specialist's office in London. The doctor's reply was genuinely warm. Congratulations on the safe arrival of a healthy daughter. The baby's grandfather made peace with his daughter and asked to see his granddaughter. Life continued on — the terror was past.

Thirty years later, similar feelings of terror caused a young woman to seek out a different kind of specialist. She, too, carried a child in her womb, and she knew that unless she made peace within herself, this child's birth would be affected.

A strange series of coincidences led her to a workshop given by a specialist who worked in the area of primal therapy. Specifically, he helped people to relive and release prenatal and natal experiences. Prompted by strong inner feelings, she found herself waiting shyly to be introduced to this man at a private home near the ocean. It was three thousand miles from the ocean where she had grown up. Driving to the town alone, she had promised herself she would leave if she felt uncomfortable. She watched intently as the doctor greeted each person. Finally, he came to shake her hand. His smile was warm and friendly. Tenderly, he bent down to touch her belly and whisper a welcome to the baby. Perhaps she could trust him.

The group of about nine people was shown an introductory film and the doctor talked about his work and research. The body holds the memories of all experiences from the moment of conception to the moment of death, he explained. Through working with his body, he had been able to relive his journey from conception to birth in movement. During this work, his body would contract in an intense physical reaction of terror at a particular stage of growth in the womb. He tried to dismiss it, but it happened again and again. Later, he verified in a conversation with his mother that she had tried to terminate his life when she was pregnant. She had never told anyone.

Listening, the young woman felt her body relax. For some time now feelings of terror had risen to the surface. She knew the source of her fear was deep, that it traced itself back to the time she spent in the womb. When she imagined herself in the womb, she would start screaming, Don't kill me...please, don't kill me, over and over, her body shaking.

The next day, there was a long therapy session. Participants were asked to lie on the floor with sheets and pillows in a dark room. Music played and the doctor moved quietly around the floor, whispering guidance and encouragement. The young woman was terrified. She wanted to run. What was she doing here anyway? He came and knelt beside her, soothing her, giving her permission to trust her body's experience. Involuntarily, her body began to express the terror and the impotence trapped in her cells for a lifetime. As the terror was released, she felt an intense aliveness, as if every cell were filled with a primal scream for life. During verbal sharing later, the others in the group listened as she haltingly tried to explain the intuition that had come to her in those moments. The primal scream uttered in the womb had been heard by her father. The doctor grinned at her happily.

In a second therapy session, the woman lay still. She was enveloped by a sense of white light surrounding the tiny body in the womb. All was protection and bliss, a state of ecstasy and delight in this tiny person. Every cell exploded with creativity and power, the power to be formed and to be birthed within this beautiful light. A feeling of oneness suffused everything. The child now in her womb and herself as a child in the womb became one. Both little children were healed and free, loved and blessed forever. For the first time in her life, the young woman experienced the source of love within her. That love had called her into life.

> It was you who created my inmost self,
> and put me together in my mother's womb;
> for all these mysteries I thank you:
> for the wonder of myself, for the wonder of your works.
> You know me through and through,
> from having watched my bones takes shape
> when I was being formed in secret,
> knitted together in the limbo of the womb.[3]

Confident serenity filled her. As if through a veil, she saw a man kneeling beside her, stroking her skin. It was as if Jesus, himself, was physically present, healing her with his touch. His love flowed into her body and spirit, empowering her to birth herself and her child. Beneath the terror of the threatened death, dwelt the life of God.

The two women in these stories each in her way came face to face with terror and the choice of life or death. Suppose a modern researcher were to offer the first woman's story as an example on a survey to test public attitudes. People could be asked to make a moral decision, based on the facts, as to what in their opinion would be in the best interests of all those involved. How many would advise an abortion, while clearly leaving the burden of choice to the mother herself? They might cite reasons of her age, the fact she could have other children, the strain of a handicapped child on a new marriage or the limited ability of a deaf, blind or physically handicapped child to enjoy life. Arguments like this are the norm in our society. The law sanctions a mother's right to make whatever decision she feels is right for her, without hearing or claim from the developing life in her womb. As a culture, we define justice. A mother has the right to choose to terminate a developing life if that life is unwanted, or imperfect, or a danger to the mental or physical health of the mother in any sense of that word. Abortion provides a swift, clinical solution to unwanted or imperfect offspring.

Likewise, if the second story were presented as factual, many people clearly would have difficulty accepting the validity of that young woman's experience. Surely, a child in the womb cannot know that it is threatened? Yet I would like to use the journeys of these two women to reveal a deeper truth. They mirror a journey the human now faces in relationship to the earth. The loving power of God, through the material nature of the earth (mater), took the unbelievable risk of birthing a species capable of seeing and celebrating beauty, but equally capable through free will of refusing to do either.

Let us, for a moment, imagine how the human appears from the earth's standpoint. The earth is mater, the material from which each of us is formed. We are children of the earth. Over the course of twenty billion years, the earth evolved life slowly, almost imperceptibly, so that conditions were ripe for the human species to emerge. And what magnificent conditions! She offers us teeming oceans, flowers, mountains, rocks, birds, every kind of animal and fish, meadows, trees, wonder upon wonder, beauty upon beauty, awesome and spectacular. With joy she births the human amid her splendor and waits to see how we shall delight in her gifts.

If we condense the twenty billion years of earth time into one year, the human has only been around for one minute. In the last seconds of that minute, we have given the earth ample reason to convince her that we are not able to celebrate her beauty or receive her gifts. Western culture is destroying them, all of them, at a rate that is so rapid our thinking cannot encompass it. The soil is being poisoned by one thousand new chemicals a year in the United States alone. All of the underground water supplies are already toxic to some degree. The air is polluted and the biosphere is beginning to show signs of breakdown. Hundreds of species of animals and plants are being destroyed each week. Weapons of mass destruction, capable of destroying the entire planet in the course of a few hours, lie hidden in her body. The human is not living in harmony with the earth process, we do not see her beauty, we do not celebrate her gifts. The human, it seems, is handicapped.

In our blindness, we bring the earth to the brink of total destruction. In our deafness, we do not hear the cries of terror from the earth as death overtakes life in so many of her life systems. In a matter of two hundred years we have perfected a way of life that today is unravelling the twenty billion years of life's gropings towards fuller and fuller expression. How can the earth continue to nurture us? Why should she? Must we not offer the mother earth the same justice that we offer the human mother? Perhaps an abortion is the most compassionate answer. Somewhere in the mind of the earth, is a choice being made to rip the human from its mother's womb in an attempt to ensure survival of life for the mother and her creatures? Is the earth finding ways to rid herself of a species that does not fit? Is the human the modern dinosaur? Is extinction inevitable?

This is terror. If beauty is the richness and preciousness of life unfolding, then its opposite is the terror that life might not continue to emerge — the terror that death might be the final statement. Death without the promise of new birth. Terror is a common experience of the human. In the beginning of human life on earth, the human lived with terror. Terror of the elements, of the majesty of the sky, of the signs and wonders in nature, led tribal peoples to create rituals and beliefs. Their terror invited humility and awe, and helped them to find ways to express gratitude. Their relationship to the earth was sacred. When terror is denied and not felt, as it seems to be so often today, it creates a blockage to life's emergence and to the full experience of life. Without humility and wonder, the earth becomes something to use, to consume and to control. There is no relationship of exchange, only one of taking what we can get.

If the earth is like the young woman whose father insisted she abort her first child because of its possible handicap, then the human today is like the child in that young woman's womb. The human needs to reconnect with the terror of that threatened child in the womb. The cultural child, the tribal-shamanic human, understood how to relate to the earth. The Native American rituals show us a people who took nothing for granted. A people who worshipped the animal they killed, gave thanks for its spirit, and the food and tools it gave them. Nothing was wasted. Rituals, like the vision quest, were journeys in which they faced their terror alone, and returned transformed to bring wisdom to the tribe. They were a people who acknowledged and praised both the Spirit who created them and the earth who nurtured them.

Terror embraced can transform the dragon of destruction. In my inner journey I know this is true. As a child I felt crippled, that I was no good. I could not stay open to that feeling and survive. I could not tell anyone. So I began to deny the terror of it by constructing a series of walls around my heart. The problem was that the defenses I used worked so well, they kept me and everyone else from knowing how I felt about myself. It became impossible for me to change or grow beyond that inner core, and slowly I stopped acknowledging any of my feelings. Instead, I chose to live rationally, and buried my emotions alive under massive defenses. The more I tried to prove to myself that I was really good, the more defensive I became. I looked good. I engaged in a host of activites to boost my self image. From the outside it all looked wonderful. On the inside there was no life.

Slowly I am uncovering the dark secrets beneath the terror. Each successive defense I built has its own terror and horror to face. It means facing the reality of who I am, and includes my shadow. My emotional denial comes at a price. I begin by admitting who I have become through my refusal to feel my terror. I am superficial. I am cruel. I am selfish. I am proud. I am greedy. I am weak. I am terrified. I am small. I am wounded. I am vulnerable. I am needy. I am sorry for the pain I have caused. I need people who are willing to share the terror of who I really am and still stay.

Thanks to many people who stayed, and to their sharing of themselves, I am learning that the terror of what I find so shameful and ugly in myself is not so unique. When I am really myself and let my pain and vulnerability show, I find that I begin to love and accept myself. Other people are drawn to me. When I remain armored and hidden, I keep people away. When I deny reality, emotional as well as rational, it is impossible to connect deeply with anyone, because I also bury my connection to myself. Once I reject myself for being too needy, weak or frightened, my heart closes and I cannot love myself or others.

Now the journey into that dark space within gives freedom. I know that the buried feelings are not the whole truth. When I choose to feel the terror, I empower myself to change. When I deny the feeling of terror, I settle for death not life. Life is present in growth. When my heart is closed and defended I stop growing.

Does this dynamic work at the cultural level? Western culture throughout history has been advanced through the destruction and domination of other peoples. Each nation has its own shameful past. America began as a nation with the mass destruction of the native peoples. For years, shiploads of black people were brought from Africa to be bought and sold like cattle. Millions of acres of untouched land were taken from the Native Americans, as white peoples destroyed their way of life and massacred the buffalo. The nation stole the Black peoples from their land, and stole the land from the Native Americans. The emotional realities of these events are well buried — they are the nation's heart secrets. Around them are built a myriad of defenses. The feelings are denied, buried alive. Around them is constructed the image of the greatest power in the world. America is the "good guy."

Since the Reformation, Western culture has worshipped reason and the intellect, while denying feelings and intuition. The valued goals are hard work and material success. The personal costs to ourselves, to families, to communities and to the earth, are seldom taken into consideration. Our heroes have been the rugged individualists who go it alone, taking what they want and being willing to step on anyone who gets in their way.

Men in this culture tend to pay a high price. Their denial of emotional needs, the inner feminine, inevitably aggravates a tendency to undervalue, or even devalue, women, the outer feminine. Competition often makes it impossible for them to have meaningful relationships with each other. Intimacy with wives, children or friends becomes lost. The physical heartache, grief and loneliness caused by their emotional isolation may erupt in heart attacks and strokes.

Women have traditionally been caretakers, providing love and nurturing. Yet no authentic value is given to the significance of their role. Breaking with tradition and achieving positions of equality within the society, often means paying the same price as men. Receptivity, vulnerability and emotional presence are rarely assets in the workplace. Modern women may thus reject their vital selves, causing their deepest needs to remain unsatisfied. The suffering of men and women is ultimately the same, the inability to value, love and express their whole persons.

Yet perhaps it is the children who suffer most. Millions of them are denied life itself. Of those who are birthed, many live through the divorce of their parents, which for them is usually a terror-filled ordeal. Where the family remains stable, many children are taken from their mothers for eight hours every day and cared for by a succession of different people. Experiments done with monkeys tell us that infants who are separated from their mothers suffer severe reactions, as do their mothers.[4] With the growth of psychology and the knowledge of the awesome power of parents to enhance or cripple children's psychological growth, are we abdicating parental responsibility rather than be the failures we perceive our parents to have been? Facing the terror of not being good enough and learning as we go is difficult. Yet from our children's perspective is it the more loving choice? Surely the presence of parents means more than all the toys and extras a paycheck provides.

To meet the material needs, which are more numerous when both parents work due to a greater consuming ability, the natural world is destroyed. Increasingly, children have no place to play where they can touch the earth. Each spring we grow a garden. A few years ago, one hot early summer day, we were turning over the soil, preparing the earth for planting. Katie, without a word, took off all her clothes, ran into the garden and began grabbing handfuls of dark brown soil, spreading it all over her body. She laughed and laughed until she fell over. Her joy at contacting the soil that nourishes her was infectious. For a moment, her skin and the skin of the earth were one. What must life be like for children who never get to play with moist earth, or lie under trees, or collapse in a pile of autumn leaves?

Many families are losing their religious roots; rituals take place at the shopping malls on Sundays rather than at the churches. There are the holy days of consumerism — the days after Christmas and Thanksgiving. Days of celebration set by the culture to honor eminent individuals have become instead days to consume. I watch the sickening disappointment on my children's faces when, having saved some money, they "go shopping." The number of choices frustrates them. The prices are nearly always out of reach. Even when their longing for a particular toy is consummated, the anticipated rush of feeling is hollow. Days later the object is discarded. It has no power to meet the deeper need.

Modern lifestyles distance children from their biological parents, from their natural parents, the earth and sky, and from their divine parents. Without parental connections, children become orphans, desparately trying to love and parent themselves in a world of instant self-gratification.

Life becomes a constant struggle for all of us to prove that we really do have self-worth, or at the collective level, national worth. What matters are appearances on every level as an individual, as a family, as a company. Keep it looking good. America is one of the richest nations on earth. Many people have fortunes. But something seems rotten at the center. In the heart lurk those dark secrets and rather than face the dragons, they are projected outward. Communism is the enemy. Hussein is the enemy. 'They" are the destructive and dominant "bad guys."

The defenses surrounding the terror are staggering. Most of us really have to struggle mentally to even begin to grasp how overwhelming the world's nuclear forces are. Western culture has valued and perfected the art of invulnerability. As with the individual personality, it has only led to insecurity. Nuclear weapons take on a new madness. Not only do they block the unfolding of life, they threaten to destroy it altogether. Can we imagine no life, no birth? Around the globe, weapons are poised to accomplish that fact.

America is one of the most heavily defended nations on earth. Her best scientific minds are employed in the business of creating ever more sophisticated and accurate weapons of mass destruction. Why is it that so many of the planet's scientists work in service to instruments of death? As a nation, America seems obsessed with defenses. Enormous amounts of money are spent to feed the obsession. During the 1980s, statistics showed that every member of the human family could have been fed, housed and medically cared for with the money America and the Soviet Union spent on armaments in a two week period.

The American lifestyle is one of luxury. The majority of Americans live to consume, and they have more to choose from in their consumption than the people of any other nation. More is better and there is always more. More homes, more cars, more money, more appliances, more food, more entertainment, more leisure, more opportunity to do everything and anything imaginable. It looks good, the American way of life.

The region of the earth known as America is beautiful. Her natural wonders are awesome. Yet across the country the beautiful places are being systematically destroyed in the name of development. The environment is being poisoned daily. The biochemistry of the planet has already been altered forever. Nuclear power plants are built while information that tells the public of their 300,000 year toxicity is ignored or repressed. Arguments against taking responsibility for acid rain are preferred to changes in industrial processes. Holes in the ozone layer of earth's fragile biosphere are reported on the inside pages of our newspapers while the death of a single human occupies the front page. A daily commute on highways choked with bumper-to-bumper cars, each one further poisoning the air we all breathe, is seen as inevitable. All these things are considered progress and progress should engender pride.

Beyond the appearance, at the heart of the American nation, what is there to see? Is life unfolding in her culture? Is this nation creative and passionate? Is she experiencing life to the fullest? If we look around, can we see life emerging? When we read our newspapers on a daily basis can we celebrate what is written there? Do you know individuals and institutions who are fulfilled, engaged in life's richness, celebrating their goodness? Are our institutions working? Do we feel a part of our government? Does our Church truly nurture us? Are we happy with the education our children receive? Is our family life conducive to raising our young in love and security? As a nation are we joyful? As a species do we love life? Do you know many individuals who are truly happy?

Is the heart of the nation inwardly paralyzed by terror, by an unconscious sense that something is deeply wrong? Do we suspect that there is more to life than a scramble to accumulate possessions and to satisfy our desires? Or that the work we are doing seems meaningless if we dare to acknowledge, even for a moment, the possibility of a nuclear end? Do we dare to feel the terror that at any moment life can be obliterated from the planet without our even being consulted? It is possible that even now the madness could have been unleashed, and this might be the last sentence you ever read? That all we own and all we give to ourselves and our children means nothing because we cannot protect them or offer them the certainty of a future? That if we stop even for a moment a sense of powerlessness and hopelessness washes over us in waves. We drown in despair.

At the root of despair lies the terror of meaninglessness. What if life has no meaning? What if death is all there is? Is the attempt to surround ourselves with material beauty and possessions a way to avoid this ultimate terror? If it is, it is not working. The price we are paying in our loss of relationship with each other and with the earth is catastrophic and even more terrifying. We must stop, turn our gaze inward and look the terror right in the eye.

I have a fantasy of an inaugural address to the nation by a new president, which goes something like this. "We are at a crucial moment in history. America is superficial. America is cruel. America is selfish. America is proud. America is greedy. America is weak. America is terrified. America is small. America is in pain. America is vulnerable. America is needy. On behalf of America I apologize to the Native American peoples, to the Black peoples, to men, women and children of our land, to all peoples in the nations whom we have exploited, to all the species that we have destroyed, to the environment that we have poisoned. We are sorry. We ask you to forgive us. We need your help as we begin to feel and face our terror, as we begin to open the heart of this nation once again."

It is a fantasy, but if we named the inner dragons and the terror they cause, transformation would begin. We could fall in love again; with ourselves, with our country, with all peoples, with our planet. We would no longer feel isolated and separate, because we would no longer need to be invulnerable and all-powerful. We would find community and the power to begin the changes we must make if we are to survive. We would be united in a common cause, joined in the struggle to save the earth and all life from destruction. As in a time of war, we could rally together as a global village to fight the enemies of nuclear end, environmental collapse, poverty and alienation. America could become one nation among many, instead of the one that has to remain on top. We could become citizens of a nation that feeds the world, instead of a nation that arms it. We could regain our true nature as a nation. The nature on which our constitution was founded, the principles of truth, equality, freedom and dignity for all life. We could discover again the spirit of the nation that joined with England and fought against evil in World War II, only this time we could unite with all nations against the evils which are threatening the earth and all her peoples. Understanding could again expand. The American Constitution used to apply only to white property owning males, then only to males, then only to males and females in the United States. Now we need to recognize the voices of all men, women and children and all the nonhuman species of the earth. All the animals and the plants, the oceans and the forests. They too must have their voice, for we are totally dependent on our connection to them for our food, our air and our water.

As I follow the way of the mother, I need to face the repressed terrors that block the flow of life from my unconscious mind. It is from the unconscious zone of the psyche that life's energy flows, the divine energy which fuels the whole cosmos. The psychic phase of the earth can be seen as the collective unconscious of which Jung spoke, and if it is, then as a species our task is to face the repressed terrors which block us from the divine energy flowing from the earth. We are cut off from that flow, and we must reconnect or continue to wither. The archetype of the Great

Mother which Marion Woodman refers to at the beginning of this chapter, is hidden in our collective unconscious; she will only reappear when we link back to, reconnect with, the divine energy of the earth, and the feminine energy of the transcendent God.

At the beginning of this chapter, I related two stories. I am intimate with the terror contained in them. The first describes my mother and father as they struggled with the decision of life or death for me, their unborn child. The young woman in the second story is myself when I was carrying Kateri in my womb. It describes my experience of facing the terror I felt in my mother's womb. Reflecting on those events and the number of connections and interactions which could have gone differently, I am returned to a state of humility and awe. My experience of those moments of resurrection and healing thirty years later, is best expressed in the words of a prayer uttered by Catherine of Siena on the Vigil of the Assumption in 1376:

> In whatever direction I turn
> I find unutterable love.
> So we can never be excused for not loving you
> for it is you alone,
> God and human,
> who loved me without my having loved you,
> for I did not exist
> and you made me.[5]

Like a tribal woman who survives a furious storm, I am put in touch with the gift of life. The terror in the womb left me feeling unsafe. It shattered the maternal matrix, the basic assumption of the child that life will provide a mother. I suffered no physical handicaps, but I was blind and deaf emotionally. In those moments of healing so many years later, I was able to reconnect with the divine energy of God. I experienced the promise given in the Scripture: "The eyes of the blind will see."[6]

That same reconnection is made every time an individual removes the blockages from the heart so as to become a vent for the fountain of divine life. Around the world, in small groups, individuals everywhere are making this journey. We find that when we share our feelings of despair and terror, they empower us and connect us to each other. In that communion we awaken to life's meaning. We begin to know intuitively that as we respond to the invitation of love, which is contained in our feelings of terror, we are changed. We recover our longing for life and the choice that we can make out of that longing, a choice for life. As each person faces his or her inner terror, it is transformed. Blind eyes are opened and see the beauty of the darkness. Deaf ears are unsealed and begin to hear the earth speaking. Whatever is transformed within the heart creates transformation for the whole. And whenever the terror of the whole is transformed, the heart is opened to a deeper experience of love.

The inner dragons truly do become princesses at the last moment with the beauty and the bravery that is needed to move us beyond our helplessness. We come to know ourselves as strands in the web of life, a web that is woven in and with and through the power of love. Working together in that truth gives life a meaning and a dignity that makes the necessary sacrifices possible.[7]

Our wounds become gifts. The journey back to the place of terror and screaming need teaches that God provides what is needed for us to choose life. When I said goodbye to the doctor who gave the primal therapy workshop, he hugged me, and asked me one question. Do you see now how important it was to feel your terror? Terror invites the heart to open to love, and an open heart filled with love can choose life. One question still remains to be answered. Will we come together and claim the love which resides in each of our hearts? The love that has groped for twenty billion years, the love that became flesh two thousand years ago, the love that is still among us finding ways to allow life to emerge. Will we claim that creativity and find ways to reverse our suicidal direction? Is our desire strong enough? Are we willing to sacrifice what we do not need in our lives and actively value what we do need: soil, water, air and the community of life? Will we listen to the earth, will we see the earth, will we speak for the earth? Will we feel the terror of possible annihilation and cry out?

If enough of us make that heart cry, I believe that God our Father will hear us, as I believe my father heard me from the womb. God our Mother, will give us the time we need to mature, to form ourselves within Her womb into a whole human, as my mother gave me. Time to birth a vision of how we can live together, celebrating our differences, while loving and protecting our common source and origin. Will we become willing to open our hearts and recover one unified primal scream for life? Will you scream with me?

CHAPTER FOUR

Death
The Transformation of Love

I call heaven and earth to witness against you today: I set before
you life and death, blessing or curse. Choose life, then, so that
you and your descendants may live, in the love of Yahweh,
your God, obeying his voice, clinging to him, for in this your
life consists, and on this depends your long stay in the land
which Yahweh swore to your fathers, Abraham, Isaac and Jacob,
he would give them.[1]

Deuteronomy 30:19-20

Facing death is the ultimate challenge of being human . . . Death
is at the heart of our being, silently calling for our transformation. In the confrontation with death, everything else is set in
perspective. In the encounter with death our soul meets divinity
and has the possibility of vowing to affirm life.[2]

Linda Shierse Leonard

Growth is measured by . . . the openness with which we continue and take the next unknown step . . . into the remarkable
mystery of being. Going beyond the mind, we go beyond death.
In the heart lies the deathless.[3]

Stephen Levine

She stared at the horror in front of her. She saw his broken body,
bruised and bleeding displayed as a spectacle. She moaned softly
and the flash of a memory played in her mind, the soft moaning
of a birth long ago. Then she had been able to cleanse and feed
his naked body, shelter him, clothe him. Simple tasks but ones
that lay forever in her heart. Now there could be no touch, no
comfort, nothing but the bodily presence of her whole being.

Her eyes never left his. Throughout his ordeal she had stayed,
affirming him with every breath, her heart flinging flames of

58

passion into his, willing him to stay connected to her love. She would not fail him now. Her mother's rage gave her a dignity which flowed from her like waves. She could not stop the madness, but her presence clearly stated that whatever the outer reality, her child was good and she loved him. Her belief in him was tangible. She knew now the treasure fashioned from her long suffering. The inner core of her was an open wound, from which flowed a love and a passion which consumed her. No one could separate her from her child. She stood rooted to the earth. Love was stronger than death.

His body was in her arms. Her heart broke open. She began to wail. Cries assailed the air, eerie sounds, piercing sounds, like those of strange and distant birds, calling from the darkness of the wood. She gave herself to her pain. Her child was dead. Tortured and abused and ridiculed, her promised one lay across her lap, lifeless. Seated on the earth, his body cradled in her arms, she rocked back and forth, howling. A woman lost in a strange world, her heart labored to birth him once again. She kissed his body again and again, a ritual of thanksgiving for all his flesh had been to her, remembering as she did so all the precious moments of his life.

Slowly she gathered herself in the present. They would wrap his body and lay him in a grave. Silently she surrendered his body to those waiting. She rose to her feet, a woman emptied and alone.

* * *

One night Albert and I were sitting in the living room talking. I was in considerable pain, and could find no rhyme or reason for the heartache. Albert intuited suddenly that whatever was going on had something to do with the miscarriage my mother had suffered when I was a year old. He told me that the dead child held a key to my healing. We prayed together for this child and immediately felt a presence in the room. Pain and longing hung in the air, as if the spirit of this lost child was begging for recognition. We named the child Angel and welcomed her into the family.

Three months later my parents came for a visit from England. I had meant to talk to them about the miscarriage but it slipped my mind, and we spent the days taking trips and enjoying being together. Mother's Day was celebrated while they were with us, and we made reservations for dinner at a local inn.

The restaurant was lovely — three floors of nooks and crannies, full of dried flowers and brass ornaments. All around the old farmhouse buildings lay the countryside of New England, radiant in the spring. We sat, three generations of the family, enjoying the special Mother's Day dinner. The food was excellent — fresh fish, baked sweet potatoes, homemade bread, all accompanied by large wooden bowls of crisp salad. After dessert, as coffee was served, my mother offered to take the girls outside to play on the swings. My father, Albert and I remained at the table.

Once we were alone, my father asked us a question. "Are you ready for a piece of family history?" I was immediately alerted by something in his tone. It had been a strange day. A friend of ours had been visiting, a Franciscan brother, and during the morning he had unpacked a box of icons and religious items on the grass outside. He explained the significance of each one, as he gave them to us. As he held up an icon of St. Nicholas, my father strode across the lawn and demanded to see it. He asked my friend if he could have it, saying that there was a story about it that he must tell me one day. I followed him into the house and pressed him to tell me, but he refused, saying he couldn't talk about it. He was clearly shaken.

Now he asked us again, "Are you sure you're ready for the past?" "Yes," I prompted him. He began haltingly. "When I saw the icon of St. Nicholas this morning, I was deeply moved, which is why I asked to have it. I told you then that I couldn't talk about the story behind it. Well, now I can. I told your mother everything earlier today feeling that she must be the first to know." He paused and looked down at the table. "You may remember that your mother suffered a miscarriage in the sixth month of her second pregnancy. She was very ill. Well, I explained to her today that the child she gave birth to was not dead, as she believed, but that her son lived for three days. Only the doctor and I knew. At my request, your mother was not told. I arranged for the child to be baptized in the hospital, and I gave him the name, Nicholas. I have never told anyone until today." I was stunned. Albert and I looked at each other in disbelief, remembering the strange and lovely moments we had shared with Angel. I told my father briefly what had happened. How we had experienced Nicholas' longing to be included in the family. My father fumbled with his coffee cup. "I honestly did what I thought was best at the time. Your mother had a terrible reaction to the medication she had to take to dry up her milk. Her body was so swollen that I could hardly recognize her when I went in to visit. It was one of the worst days of my life. I felt she simply couldn't handle anymore suffering. We knew the baby would die, it was only a matter of time."

We continued to talk. As we rose to leave, my father cautioned me, "Don't mention this to your mother. She's pretty shocked and I think it's best you don't bring it up." It was a familiar warning.

We piled into the car and began the ride home through steepled villages following the path of the swift-flowing river. Seated in the back with my mother, the girls between us, I stole a glance at her face. She was staring out of the window, her expression set and grim, muscles tense as she held herself together. As the car pulled into the driveway of our house and we got out, I followed her into the garden. Without a word I put my arms around her and she collapsed against me sobbing. "I never touched him . . . or held him . . . I never saw his face. I never nursed him . . . I had so much milk . . . so much milk . . . so much milk," she wailed. Her only memory of her son was watching a nurse put him in a plastic bucket and carry him out of the room.

We stood there in the overgrown garden, crying together. Amid the tears was joy and laughter, a son, a brother. A new son on Mother's Day after all these years. My mother told me that all her married life she had dreams of a child dying whom she could never reach in time. "Now I understand." The tears flowed once more. Nicholas had come home at last.

The next day, the final day of their visit, I took a walk with my father on a nearby college campus. We wandered through the grounds, admiring the cherry trees in blossom, talking of many things. We stopped next to a cornfield and sat facing each other on huge rocks, while my father smoked a cigarette. As we walked back up the hill, my father ventured the subject of Nicholas.

"As you know, Carol, I'm not a religious man, but I do want you to know that I have tried in my own way to make peace with him. I feel guilty knowing that Nicholas may have suffered all these years because of my decision to keep his life a secret. I've carried the burden of that secret every day of my life since then. I knew I should tell your mother but the time never seemed right. I wondered if I'd go to my death carrying it."

We reached the car and climbed in. My father turned to me and said quickly, "I do love you, you know." It was the first time in my memory that he had said those words.

Those days are precious memories. The tender connection with both my mother and my father was a new experience. When they returned home to England they checked into records of Nicholas' birth and death. My father was shocked to discover that his memory was mistaken. The child had been christened Nigel, the name my mother would have chosen, not Nicholas which was his choice. Nigel apparently had tried to tell us who he was and we had mistakenly chosen the name Angel, so close to Nigel in sound. Nigel had in fact died after one day of life, not three. Had my father's memory been clear, the icon of St. Nicholas might never have caught his attention and set in motion such a strange and wonderful series of events.

My father's decision to tell us the truth was an opening for the whole family. The denial of Nigel's life and death affected all of us. It blocked the flow of love between my parents, between my father and myself and between my father and my brothers and sister. How can you hold the pain of one child's death within your heart without having that unexpressed pain affect your love for your living children? The only way I know is to keep your heart defended and thus the expression of your love for everyone around you must be diminished. How can you keep a secret of that depth from the woman you share your life with unless you maintain a barrier around that inner place where the secret lives. Nigel was buried alive along with the grief and the pain his death caused, and that denial diminished the radiance of our family.

Yet the release and affirmation of that buried life and death had a profound effect. When my father shared his secret with us and we welcomed Nigel into our family, something changed. Nigel, with his presence, infused the family with new life, bringing love and connections that went deep. Perhaps we could not have received him before, and he has been willing to wait to give us his gift: the promise of new life.

Life and death are intimately related. The arrival of one heralds the possibility of the other. The possibility of my baby dying was something I had to consider before I gave birth at home. I heard a midwife say that if her baby were to die, she would want to be at home, free to grieve and hold his body until she was able to let him go. Death, like birth, is so often hidden or avoided. Efficient professionals take care of the body and spare family members from too much reality. I remember my parents' shocked response when my ten-year-old brother asked to see his grandmother's body after she had died. It was out of the question.

When we relinquish choices about birth and death, we no longer enter fully into their mystery. Increasingly we are not truly born, nor do we truly die, because we are not passionately present to the moment. Instead we move unconsciously through these awesome rites of passage. We are passively pulled into life by sterile equipment or passively manipulated to remain in life by equally sterile equipment, lacking at every step the freedom to participate fully in our own birth or death. I remember the sight of my first corpse at a wake. Wakes had not been a ritual in the society I grew up in and I stared in horror at the rosy unreality of the "mask" in the coffin. Here was the epitome of "painting a smile on a corpse."

I have needed to grieve my tiny brother's death, to mourn the longing I still have to have seen his body, to have touched him, to have said "hello" and welcomed him, so that I could have said "goodbye." In doing so, my heart has opened to many other griefs and losses, to many other people I never said "goodbye" to in my life. The pain has softened my heart and made it bigger. Nigel is now present to me. The gift of his life cannot be measured by the number of hours that his body breathed, but only by the amount of love and energy which flowed through his being and still flows. His death was in no way an ending.

In order to fully choose life for myself, I need to face death. As I ponder in my heart about death, I sense that dying has to do with becoming willing to relinquish control. After I turned thirty, I began to realize that all the disciplines, roles, structures and schedules in my day cannot save me from death, or from life. The choice to live fully is a choice to live in the unknown moment and to trust it. I know I face that realization daily and try to stay open to what is, rather than to escape into what I wish would be. To remain present to the moment is to accept death; to let my expectations go; to live with the paradox of beauty and terror, birth and death, and to simply accept and experience what is given.

One Saturday morning in early summer we were getting ready to go away for the weekend. I told Albert we must stop on the way and visit his mother in a nursing home. He refused, but I kept insisting. He kept refusing. Finally, to get me off his back, he agreed. Taking Katie with us we made our way down the corridor to my mother-in-law's room. She was in great distress, nervously tugging at the tubes taped to her arms and hands. She knew us, however, and smiled at Katie saying over and over what a beautiful child she was. Her hair was wild and she looked like a crazy woman, fingers moving incessantly, her mind wandering. I went close to the bed and began to stroke her forehead. "I'm so tired" she wailed, "so tired." "You can go to sleep now, Memere, it's okay, you're quite safe. You can go to sleep now." She lay back on her pillows and nodded. We said goodbye and continued on our journey.

When we returned two days later there was a message from the nursing home. Albert's mother had died an hour after we left. The nurse had brought her a milkshake which she drank and then she fell asleep peacefully.

Death's greatest terror is that its mystery is faced alone. My horror for Nigel is that he lay alone without a touch or a word to encourage him on his journey. Death forces me to relinquish my connections at least on the physical realm with everyone I love. The agony for my brother is that he had so few to let go of. Yet that is his gift to me; it clearly tells me that the denial of death is the real enemy because it keeps me from making, valuing, and deepening my connections with those I love. My fear closes up my heart, and once closed, I cannot be a channel of love and connection. If I accept death, talk about it, listen to and honor my feelings about it, I can allow my heart to be torn open, I can treasure the love and the pain that I feel and offer it freely in each moment that I have. Love becomes the bridge between death and life. Life becomes precious.

A neighbor of mine, a young woman, was killed recently by a drunk driver. She was nine and a half months pregnant with her third child and her two sons were with her in the car. She and her soon to be born baby boy died instantly and were trapped in the car for some time while the rescue squads worked to free them. Her sons lived through it. Her wake and funeral were agonizing. I shall never forget the faces of her sons as they followed her coffin down the aisle, or the three red roses on the side of her coffin with her boys' names on them. The terrible mystery of death filled the room, turning lives upside down and filling our hearts with questions that cannot be answered.

Being willing to be open to the feelings I have inside me often feels like death. Tragedies and daily incidents in relationships trigger memories of abandonment or experiences of unmet needs from childhood. Sometimes it seems I will die if I feel them. But, I find that as my heart opens to death and life, I become rooted in the vast web of living and non-living beings, and I see that when I allow myself the experience of death, I connect more deeply with life. When I physically die the web of life will not collapse or disappear. My physical body will no longer be a synapse through which love passes, but the essence of my heart or soul, the source of the connection, will remain, as Nigel, Memere and my neighbor have remained.

Perhaps the earth is covered with a vast spider's web through which the loving energy of God flows. At every point of intersection there is a synapse, either physical or spiritual, in a particular form. That form of Being can either allow the love to flow through, or it can stop it. Those who cannot consciously welcome all the experiences of life, including death, will become synapses no longer capable of transmitting energy to the whole web. The divine flow is blocked.

The inner journey is about removing the blockages to that flow of love. The blockages are like bands around the heart. In the fairy tale of "The Frog King, or Iron Henry" the coachman Henry rides behind the carriage which takes the girl and her prince to his kingdom. When the wicked witch turned his master into a frog. "Faithful Henry had been so unhappy . . . that he had caused three iron bands to be laid round his heart, lest it should burst with grief and sadness." Now, "full of joy" because the spell has been broken, they journey home. The King's son hears a noise like something breaking and asks Henry if it is the carriage.

"No, master, it is not the carriage. It is a band from my heart, which was put there in my great pain when you were a frog and imprisoned in the well." Again and once again while they were on their way something cracked, and each time the King's son thought the carriage was breaking; but it was only the bands which were springing from the heart of faithful Henry because his master was set free and was happy."[4]

As the bands around the heart break open, there is both new life and death. A part of the self must die, and it hurts. However keenly I understand the need to give up a behavior which is keeping me from growth, I mourn its loss and everything in me battles against its death. Each "steel band" that breaks opens me to a deeper connection with life, an intimacy which terrifies as well as beckons. Each band has been placed there for self-protection, to help me to deny my grief and my vulnerability, and to break it open is to die a little.

Yet the inner poverty of a broken heart is where the power of love can work. Love cannot be possessed, it can only be received, and only hearts that have been hollowed out have the capacity to receive love. Hearts with steel bands around them only block love's entry. Being vulnerable is the way of the mother. A mother knows that the seed of new life brings death. Death of freedom, death of the ability to choose her own needs, death of the idea that she possesses her body. As mother I welcome those deaths, even while I struggle against them. I bring this new person forth, another death as I push the fruit of my womb from my body; I nourish this body with my milk, a death of all and every plan, and I love this body/soul, feel with her, grow with her, comfort her, and slowly die a little each time I teach her to move away from me. As I birth my child, I know that my child will see my death or that I will see my child's death. Birth creates death.

As mother I am responsible to offer myself compassion. The times when I contact and relive childhood feelings can be horrific. It is as if the child inside me must die in order to be reborn. How I fight the process! When I allow that little girl to be in my heart, I feel that her pain will kill me. Years of abandonment and unexpressed longing well up, threatening to choke me. I have cried tears which led to rages, tantrums which led to more tears. I know I need to allow that part of myself to exist. I needed to confront my parents to try and get for her what she was screaming for, but her needs are overwhelming and I am no longer a child.

Accepting my memories and the death of my illusion that I can change them is a life work. Part of the dying process is to learn to receive and to treasure what is given in the present. I can choose life now and allow what love there can be for today. There will always be empty spaces but it is those spaces that can be offered as vessels for love.

I realize how important it is for me to grieve my inner deaths. As I surrender to the power of God and allow Love to flow into me, I can begin to love and nurture my inner child. Slowly I die to the belief that someone "out there" will make her happy. Death does put everything in perspective and allows me to mother the seed of the child who can choose life, who can be with its mystery in wonder, and can spontaneously play with its unfolding.

It is this divine child who can choose life for the mother, the earth. The earth is dying. Daily she suffers unprecedented deaths; entire species become extinct, one every twenty minutes, while scientists struggle to name them so that at least there is a record of their existence. Like Nigel, their lives and deaths remain secrets from most of the human family. Daily about 100,000 humans starve to death on our planet, 40,000 of them are babies. This figure does not include the thousands of others who continue to live a malnourished and diminished existence without even minimal comfort or shelter. Each year huge areas of tropical rain-forests are decimated and scientists estimate that at the present rate of destruction, not taking into account increased populations, there will be no forests left in about thirty years. With those forests die countless species of plant and animal life whose beauty and value will never be known. With those forests dies the earth's ability to produce oxygen, the life-breath of so many of her species.

Many people in governments all over the world have chosen, as my father did, to keep these deaths a secret. They make us uncomfortable and if we open our hearts to the truth of them, we experience pain and terror. It becomes impossible to approve of the continued destruction of the planet as a normal and neces-sary part of progress. Once we feel the facts, things change. More and more members of the human family are beginning to learn these secrets. Individuals everywhere are beginning to embrace these deaths and the knowledge of these deaths. As we do, a new possibility is created. We find that we can come together and begin to find ways to affirm and protect life.

As Linda Leonard promises, when I face the deaths that are taking place everywhere today in the life systems of the planet, I hear the voice that the dying sing, a voice that is silently calling for transformation. It is the same voice with which Nigel called to me before I knew his story. When I close my ears, my mind and my heart so as to avoid feeling the terror and pain that the voice brings, I do not confront death and I do not change. I do not set my life in perspective, I do not recognize that for me and for my children and for their children to live, the earth must live and unfold in radiance. I do not learn that her biological diversity is our strength and our survival, and that the human can and must live as one species among many. I do not meet the divine mystery, and I do not discover my life's possibility nor the transforming power that I have in my vow to affirm life.

Facing this death means relearning how to live. I am learning how to give my life as food for the future. If I can become someone who receives the energy of evolution in the same way that a nerve ending receives energy from the brain, who opens to it, infuses it with my unique spark of life, and encourages it to leap forward to the next being in the web, I will be giving my life to the whole. I experience moments of this, when I am on fire with the excitement of participating in an emerging cosmos. I am in touch with my gift, the gift that every being has, for the whole. My life and my energy become food, nourishment for the entire system. I pass the messages I am entrusted with through my heart and thus allow my body and my greater Body to work in harmony.

When out of fear and terror I close my heart, preferring to remain withdrawn or obsessed with activity, I no longer hear the inner voice and I die as a living synapse. Imagine for a moment that the whole earth is a Body and imagine yourself as a nerve synapse in the middle finger of her right hand. Every time the message from the brain is sent to that finger to press a letter on my keyboard, the message is stopped. The energy gets as far as the hand but cannot jump into the finger because your synapse is no longer a living point of connection for the flow of energy. The Body can adapt. It can type using only the second and fourth fingers of the right hand, but its ability to create will be diminished. Eventually the finger will atrophy from lack of life and energy and will become paralyzed. The Body will have died a little.

When death is denied by a culture, the facts about how much of the earth's Body has already died must also be denied. No pain is felt for the loss of species, nor reflection given to the fact that their role in the Body is gone forever. The feelings which would connect us to the Body of the earth are repressed along with the reality of how sick she is.

In *The Prophetic Imagination* Walter Brueggemann describes Jesus' life as the primary example of prophectic ministry. In studying the Beatitudes, the seminal teachings of Jesus, we come to in Brueggemann's words:

> no more succinct summary of prophetic ministry than . . . "Blessed are you that weep now, for you shall laugh!" (Luke 6:21), or more familiarly, "Blessed are those who mourn, for they shall be comforted!" (Matt. 5:4). Jesus' concern was, finally, for the joy of the kingdom. That is what he promised and to that he invited people. But he was clear that the rejoicing in that future required a grieving about the present order . . . . There is work to be done in the present. There is grief work to be done in the present that the future may come.[5]

This grief work is the reponsibility of all of us. It is hard and painful. But until it is done, there is no room in the heart for the comfort that Jesus promises, for the new way, for the joy of the kingdom. Watching my husband, Albert, grieve the deaths of his parents over the last few years gives me a sense of the magnitude of the grieving we must do as a species. Yet it is the only authentic path to joy. To quote Brueggemann further:

> The mourning is a precondition in another way too. It is not a formal, external requirement but rather the only door and route to joy . . . Only that kind of anguished disengagement permits fruitful yearning and only the public embrace of deathliness permits newness to come. We are at the edge of knowing this in our personal lives, for we understand a bit of the processes of grieving. But we have yet to learn and apply it to the reality of society.[6]

And I would add, we have yet to apply it to the reality of our home, the planet earth. Grieving removes the blockages of denial around our hearts. It opens us to become vulnerable. Public grieving awakens others to the deaths taking place on our planet. In the same way that grieving the deaths of the inner journey snaps open the bands around the heart, so the human journey can be about the same process. As a species we can break the steel bands that separate us from the life systems of the planet, so that we can feel again our connection to the processes of the body of the earth. It means facing death; the death of our control over the body of the earth, the death of the idea that the earth's resources are a possession for our needs alone, the death of our pride, the hubris of the human, and the death of our illusion of self-sufficiency. It is by living lives in harmony with the earth's life systems that we discover the kingdom of joy.

This is the reality that is at work throughout the cosmos. Life's power is in its connection and relationship to itself in all its many forms. The human cannot experience joy as a species until we recognize that meaning and peace exist only when we are sharing the flow of life with everything else that lives, giving and receiving, protecting and being protected, nurturing and being nurtured by the mystery of life. It is time for an age of true stewardship, where the human "fits" into the earth systems and guides and protects the unfolding of life in all its diversity and beauty.

Natural death is part of the mystery of life. It is a creation of evolution, an invention of the cosmos. It is the way of the earth: constantly allowing the seeds of life to grow, blossom and die, then absorbing their dying back into her Body to nourish her so that new life may be brought forth. As I journey as mother I become willing to meet with death. I allow death to be my companion, my teacher on the way. I learn to appreciate the rich fertility of the seasons. The magnificence of the dying earth in the fall. The willingness of all things to "fall" back into the earth so that they may nourish her. There is the long dark wait as life reshapes itself, hidden from the light. And then there is the startling rebirth which amazes with its beauty. Death has its beauty.

As a species we are altering this pattern biologically, and even geologically. We are playing with evolution and dramatically changing the life systems of the planet, without any sense of how or even if the earth can adapt to what we do. We are stripping death's beauty from the cosmos. We are introducing unnatural death that is not within the greater movement of evolution; death that is bizarre and violent; death that we do not know how to mourn, for we have yet to even acknowledge it. We are introducing death that does not have the ability to nourish the earth and continue the cycle of rebirth because it is forced unnaturally on the planet in a way that makes it impossible for her life systems to adapt to its sudden violence. Imagine burning your arm. The pain goes away and the skin heals over time, often leaving no scar. But if your arm is covered with gasoline and set fire there is a point at which the body can no longer heal itself or return its skin and structure to their original beauty and creativity. This is what we are doing to the earth's Body.

On my inner journey I meet the tyrannical child, uncover her true needs, grieve and allow her to die. The human species needs to do the same. We cannot have everything that we have trained ourselves to want. We cannot demand to use what amounts to 40 percent of the earth's total terrestrial photosynthetic productivity for our own consumption without giving equal energy to fostering the earth's new life. We cannot allow so many of our species to die without food or shelter, while a few live lives of luxury. We must begin to name the selfish superficiality of so much of our lives and begin to face the necessary death of our unending consumption. We have to face the death of our illusions, and grieve publicly and prophetically, so that the possibility that reality now offers us can be embraced. We must enter the dying process so that we may be reborn.

The human has brought the earth to an unnatural season of fall, and we are heading rapidly towards an unnatural winter. In this reality of death lies an unprecedented opportunity for a new vision for our species to be birthed. We have a chance to learn what we have always struggled to learn, how to live together, how to be connected to each other, how to be in touch with the earth, how to live. By acknowledging the enormity of the death we are inflicting on our home, and expressing our grief and our outrage, we begin to change. Out of the depths to which our grief can bring us, we can awaken to the mystery, the vast energy, the divinity, which is moving through the universe. A mother's grief and rage at a child's death is an awesome power. Feeling the grief of the earth births that power. That power can heal the earth.

God's message to the people of the Old Testament is before us still. Today, we need more than at any time in history to discover how we can choose Life, how we can actively say "Yes!" to the future. I believe we will only make that choice when we become willing to confront Death as the only other alternative. We are a culture whose denial of death has created a love of death, whose repression of death forces us to play with death and run headlong toward it unconsciously. We must stop and confront death, look into the face of nuclear annihilation, discover the facts about the earth's deaths, feel the poisoning of our water, our air and our soils, and behold the eyes of the starving children. Death does put things in perspective. Grief forces each of us to ask what is important, what matters, what endures. It beckons us toward transformation and the meeting with the Divine for which we long. Death asks the questions all of us must answer for ourselves. When we do we will find our own possibility, our own vow, our own affirmation of Life.

On our wedding day, my husband had promised to visit a friend of his who was too ill from a muscular disease to attend the chapel. I had never met this man and was somewhat embarrassed and awkward at the thought of our visit. I entered the room where he lay grinning in a hospital bed. I was overwhelmed by the peace there. We spoke a little and he gave us a wedding gift he had waiting beside him. He was very weak. As we were leaving I drew close to the bed to say goodbye. He began to try to raise himself up off his pillows so he could kiss me. Instead of giving into my temptation to lean forward and make it easy for him, I waited. With tremendous effort he inched himself up by pulling on the steel bars at either side of his bed. He gave me a strong kiss and sank back smiling. I clearly remember that moment. That man's dignity and the gift of his kiss lives on in me. He died while we were on our honeymoon.

Each of us has a gift which Love asks us to add to Her flow as she spirals throughout the cosmos. If during our time of physical life, we can empty our hearts, the Love flowing through us will be transformed and enriched with our gift. We will be one with the mother earth, busy with the work of bearing fruit, that we may be food for others. Then once our fruit has been plucked and eaten by eager mouths, we can sink again into the Body of our Mother, nourishing her with our bodies, that they too may be fertile food for the future.

CHAPTER FIVE

Creativity
The Outpouring of Love

The creative process has a feminine quality, and the creative work arises from unconscious depths — we might truly say, from the realm of the Mothers.[1]

Carl G. Jung

You must give birth to your images. They are the future waiting to be born . . . fear not the strangeness you feel. The future must enter into you long before it happens . . . just wait for the birth . . . for the hour of new clarity.[2]

Rainer Maria Rilke

Modern woman must discriminate and relate to the image of the spirit, while at the same time maintaining her roots in her basic feminine nature — that which receives, nourishes, and gives birth on all levels of being through her awareness of the earth and her ability to bring up the water of life from under the earth. All her true creativeness springs from this . . . the woman who quietly responds with intense interest and love to people, to ideas, and to things, is as deeply and truly creative as one who always seeks to lead, to act, to achieve.[3]

Helen M. Luke

She sat in silence. Her emptiness allowed her to absorb all the feelings in the room. She studied the precious faces around her. All had aged; grief had etched its way into their skin. The man next to her gazed at the floor, his whole body slumped forward in defeat. She longed to comfort him but there was no way to ease this loss. The pain and terror of these days was like a tornado, destroying everything in its path, shattering every structure of the mind, leaving it an empty plain of desolation. Each one dwelt in consuming darkness alone.

One by one bitter memories assailed them, torturing their very selves, leaving them stripped and battered. All they had been and done haunted them incessantly, reducing each of them to where they now sat, huddled together, full of self-loathing, abandoned and bereft. Despair filled the air with a howling hopelessness.

She prayed silently, letting herself sink as she had done so many times to be within the bloody center of herself. She knew from years of patiently willing herself to be there that the wound never bled in vain. It mattered not that she understood what was happening. She had never known that luxury. Only one thing was necessary — the simple offering of the wounded heart to God. She knew that these men and women were seeing inside themselves, perhaps for the first time. Everywhere they looked, they saw the brokenness of their hearts, the abysmal failures of their attempts to love. Offer it all, she pleaded wordlessly; accept, surrender. Be willing to receive the love, be willing to receive, be willing, be.

Powerful energy began to move from heart to heart. Bodies and minds centered themselves. Groping hands reached out to clasp another, until a tangible love flowed through them all. It grew in intensity, penetrating the darkness, exposing their arid desert places. No one spoke. They held the tension of the waiting — alert, transformed, offering the empty crucible of their circle as a gift.

She felt a sudden burning desire ignite her heart and mind. Long ago she had felt that same consuming touch enter her. Now a radiant flame lit up her emptiness, and roared around the circle like a forest fire, gathering up into its heat all doubt and shame, leaving in its path fertile ashes of new life. Her heart sang, a soaring knowing filled her. Suddenly, the room was filled with sound. Men and women released all the passion they could no longer contain. Love dwelt among them. She rejoiced inwardly. She was no longer alone. Her secret lover was unleashed upon the earth.

*   *   *

Seven years ago Albert, Becky and I moved from New England to California. We drove across the country with only the belong-ings we could fit in the car. We had no home when we arrived, no one we knew, no security. Two weeks after we arrived I turned thirty, which seemed to signal the beginning of a creative period for me. Life was turned upside down. Dreams became a channel for the images I needed to bring to birth.

The most important dream had occurred at least a year before. In it I was sitting in a house with French windows. An old woman dressed in black, carrying shopping baskets, came to the window and peered in. She was cross-eyed and appeared mad. I was extremely frightened and felt she wanted to get me. I woke up in terror.

A second dream shortly afterward took place in the same room. I was sitting and talking with a friend, a pleasant gentle woman. As we talked, a child came to the window and began knocking. She was trying to get our attention. I told my friend she was there. My friend denied it. I insisted that she look at her. She refused. I started yelling at her that the child wanted to come in. She continued to behave as though the child didn't exist. I woke up as I was running across the room toward my friend, pleading with her and shaking her roughly to make her look at the child. She would not acknowledge her.

The images in these two dreams were extremely powerful. They remained with me though I did not understand them. A month after arriving in California, I received two more dreams. The first took place in an old underground mine, full of passageways. I was looking for something and felt I was in danger, that someone was after me. I found a brown paper bag. Inside were my brother's hands, cut off at the wrist.

A few nights later I dreamt that I saw my daughter, then age two, on a bicycle. She was out of control. When I caught sight of her, she was rounding a corner. I was in the back of a car going in the opposite direction and I spent the rest of the dream trying to reach her. My progress was incredibly slow meeting with numerous obstacles, but finally reaching the street into which I had seen her disappear. She was dead. Someone had lain her on a raised pyre surrounded by lighted candles. I awoke in terror.

With the help of a guide, I began to explore the images in the latter two dreams. We interpreted the dreams by seeing each character as a part of myself. The hands of my dead brother symbolized my creativity. The dream pointed to the danger I was in of destroying that creativity; of severing it from myself. A few weeks before the dream, a friend had given me a small statue of Mary, a gift to her from her grandmother. I was having great trouble sleeping and she sent it to comfort me. After the dream, I noticed that both Mary's hands were missing.

At the same time, I started to read a book which analyzed the fairy tale, "The Girl Without Hands." This gave me further insight into my dream and the whole process of creativity. It is now a favorite story which gives me courage during the dark times of birthing.

In the story, a poor miller is out in the forest chopping wood one day. A man approaches and promises him great riches in exchange for what lies behind his mill. Thinking it to be only his apple tree, the man gives his written agreement. The man tells him that he will collect what belongs to him in three years' time. Returning home, the miller discovers that his only daughter had been standing behind the mill when he made the promise. He had sold his daughter to the Devil.

Three years later the Devil comes to claim the girl. She washes herself clean with water and draws a circle around herself. The Devil cannot approach her. Furious, he orders her father to keep all water from his daughter. He returns a second time, but the girl's tears wash her hands clean and again he is powerless to possess her. Then the Devil insists that her father cut off his daughter's hands, or else he will have no power over her. In terror, the father obeys him. Again his daughter weeps and her tears flow so freely onto the stumps of her wrists that they become quite clean. The Devil returns a third time. He still has no power over her and this time he gives in. The maiden is free.

Her father offers to take care of her with his riches from the Devil, but she chooses to go into the forest alone. Tying her maimed arms behind her back, she sets out on her journey. As night approaches she sees a garden full of fruit trees, but it is surrounded by water. Being faint with hunger, and despairing of her way, she falls to her knees in prayer. An angel appears and makes a path through the water so she can enter the garden. She eats a piece of fruit from one of the trees. The garden belongs to a King who is informed of the missing fruit and the mysterious intruder. The King keeps watch the following nightfall. When the maiden comes to eat, he speaks to her and she tells him her story.

He falls in love with her and marries her, promising to take care of her. He makes her a pair of silver hands.

Later the King is called away on a journey and he leaves his bride in the care of his mother. While he is gone the Queen gives birth to a son and his mother sends a joyous message to the King announcing this good news. The Devil exchanges the messages between them, and the King receives word that his wife has given birth to a monster. He, nonetheless, responds telling his mother to take great care of the Queen. Again, the Devil changes the letter, this time sending a message from the King telling his mother to kill his wife and son. Later false messages tell her to cut out the maiden's heart and keep it in a box for his return. The mother is unable to destroy them and tells the Queen to leave with her newborn son. The maiden ties her child on her back and returns again to the forest. Once more, in answer to her prayer, an angel comes and leads her to a small house, bearing a sign over the door which reads "here all dwell free." She spends seven years there and during this time "by God's grace, because of her piety, her hands which had been cut off, grew once more."

The King returns home and when he learns the truth from his mother, he sets out vowing to neither eat nor drink until he finds his wife and son. For seven years he "sought her in every cleft of the rocks and every cave." Finally, he comes to the house in the woods where the maiden lives with their son, Sorrowful. At first the King is not sure that this is indeed his bride, because she has hands of flesh and blood, but the angel brings him her silver hands and he recognizes her. He kisses them, saying:

> A heavy stone has fallen from my heart. Then the angel of God ate with them once again, and after that they went home to the King's aged mother. There were great rejoicings everywhere, and the King and Queen were married again, and lived contentedly to their happy end.[4]

This story resonates deeply with my way. My father unwittingly sold my creativity to the devil by denying his own. I was now facing the choice of either defying the devil through surrender to God, or continuing to be a victim by remaining my father's little girl. My defiance required that I begin to open up my feelings (the maiden's tears), take my own side and be willing to stand alone. My dream was telling me that my hands had already been cut off. Only my tears could save me from being claimed by the devil. If I continued to play the role of victim both to my father and to the devil I would abort my creativity and, in fact, my personhood.

The second dream confirmed this. The child, so out of control, died. Even though much of my psyche tried to save her, I was too late. The woman who was guiding me suggested that the dream was positive. The helpless child whose life needed the control of others had died. I was ready to give up my dependency. I could now choose to take responsibility for my life.

I felt as though my psyche was undergoing earthquakes. My personality, the fundamental assumptions I had built about who I was, crumbled. A course I was taking helped me to name the process. In it we explored the evolution of the universe. The instructor encouraged us to see how our unfolding followed the stages of the earth's unfolding. Continental plates within were shifting, wreaking havoc on the surface! My "ice age" was passing, giving way to a flood of tears as the ice caps around my heart began to melt.

Using a process of active imagination enabled me to contact figures in my dreams. The two people in the garden in my early dreams emerged strongly. I had to confront and begin to communicate with the woman in black, whom I named Hag. She was terrifying. She represented all the things I had refused to face within myself — darkness, madness, aloneness and death. As we talked, she began to show me another face. Beneath her ugly exterior was a part of myself I had rejected. Lack of love and nurturing had aged and abused her. Now she was tapping on the window of my home, trying to get my attention. She wanted to come in to the house of my self. Gradually I learned to love her and finally to embrace her. I wrote a poem at that time:

SISTER

You are my lost sister
Old face pressed against the window
Eyes staring, crossed and crazy
Dressed in black you walk the streets
Your shopping bags full of smothered children.

My house is bigger now

My heart is giving birth
Tearing with each contraction
Opening to let you in
I want to bring you home
to soothe away your wrinkles
to kneel before your gaze
to kiss your blood red lips
I want to love you sister
I want to make the babe leap in your womb.[5]

One afternoon while sitting in a rocking chair, I imagined a dialogue with Hag. I knew then I had to invite her in to my "house." She was afraid. She did not trust me. I prayed. A figure, my image of Jesus, appeared. Picking her up (she was still outside the house in the garden) he carried her gently into the house. She was close to death. He laid her on a bed and taking her hand in his, murmured the words "Talitha cum, talitha cum." She sat up, no longer an old woman but a child. Hag and the child in the garden that appeared in my dreams were one. My rejection of my inner child, my refusal to acknowledge her, had turned her into an ugly old woman. Once I began to love her again, she could be reborn as a child.

My husband, Albert, had guided me during my conversations with Hag. In many ways he was the King in the fairy tale who had fallen in love with me and given me silver hands. I was, like the maiden in the tale, wandering lost and alone when I met him, starving for spiritual food. I enthusiastically entered marriage, enchanted by my husband's deep love for me and his vision. He offered images of a life I had never experienced. His passionate creativity allured me. My support of his work and my sharing of his vision were my silver hands.

As my inner life began to explode, and my own images came to birth, I had to symbolically return to the forest. God became my comforter and I had to enter the house where "all dwell free." I needed to be with my inner child whose name was surely Sorrowful, so that I could pay attention to her and give her the freedom she needed. I also had to allow flesh and blood hands, my own creativity, to grow. It took a long time of patient waiting. Resenting and blaming Albert for having what I did not have was the most tempting solution! But I could not cut off his hands to keep him bound to me. I had to wait and trust in God's grace and the earth's nurturance and believe that if I attended to Sorrowful and took care of my pain and grief, new growth would emerge.

Albert helped with many of my inner dialogues during this time. He was struggling with inner figures in his own psyche. One in particular we talked about. We named him Animal; a figure representing all the rage and violence repressed from the abuse of his own childhood. He, like the King, was off on his own journey and our communication was often interceded by the Devil. Only our trust in God kept us faithful. In the tale, it is the mother who saves the life of the Queen by refusing to obey the false messages of destruction. The mother, the unconscious realm, is where the truth lies. The creative work as Jung says, arises from "the realm of the Mothers." During this time, despite the outward reality, we had to trust intuitively in the original vision of our marriage. I had to wait to allow the lost parts of myself to heal and Albert had to find his way to the inner feminine. The statue of the handless Mary became an important meditation image.

One night Albert encouraged me to express the rage that Hag felt. Screaming and pounding on his chest, my anger erupted, followed by hot tears of agony. Spontaneously while I was consciously being Hag, Albert suggested that we enter into a marriage between the unconscious figures who were emerging in us. Solemnly we removed our wedding rings and he took vows to Hag, and I to Animal, promising to love and to cherish each other forever. It gave us permission to be the whole of who we are and to know that we are loved. The moment was deeply charged with grace and acceptance. We cried and laughed and consummated our love, more deeply connected to ourselves and to each other than ever before. The fairy tale "The Girl Without Hands" ends with the King and Queen remarrying. Our remarriage was a new birth for each of us. It allowed Albert to expose the pain and terror which was hidden beneath his raging Animal, and it allowed me to own my lost rage and creativity, my abandoned child who was buried as Hag.

All those images are still coming to birth in me today. It is not an event that happened then, but a process that continues daily as I learn to be with my inner child and to welcome and birth Hag's creativity. Recently during meditation I asked the question, "where are you Hag?" because I was experiencing anger and rage and I needed to know she was there. An image of a strong, dark middle-aged woman, fiery and powerful appeared, smiling at me knowingly.

Again and again I receive the teaching that it is from the depths that creativity comes, and that if I do not enter my depths, be it pain, anger or sadness, my creativity will not be sparked. It is when I journey inward and discover my wounds, that I find I can live through, with, and in them. In the wound is the power I need to love and to create. Pain gives birth to that power. Vulnerability gives birth to creativity. When I labor in that dark space within, as I did during the year in California, fear eventually gives birth to courage, and despair gives birth to hope. As I accept my wounds and surrender them to God, I become willing to be used.

Our marriage is now ten years old. My hands are strong and flexible. I write with them, hands of flesh and blood, not artificial silver. I still love and support Albert's vision and love the passion of his creativity, but I also cherish my images and the miracle of my own hands. My continuing journey into sorrow and darkness and my times in the forest, show me how to dwell in freedom. The process of birth, death, and rebirth continues.

The earth confirms this process. As humans, we now know the story of the unfolding of life from the beginning of time. It seems that the entire universe was born from the dark. In the beginning there was nothing, and then, out of that fecund darkness, a giant explosion of light erupted. That explosive moment contained the potential of everything we now name as existing in the universe. It also contained everything we have not yet named. Each atom that is present in my body, the earth, the solar system, the galaxy, and the entire universe was present, in potential within that unfolding of creativity. The darkness which preceded the light was a plenary emptiness, for it is an emptiness which is full of creativity, the mysterious power of life waiting to be evoked. This story reminds me that I make the same journey. The dark emptiness which I carve out inside as I mine my wounds, is a plenary emptiness and it is out of that fecund darkness that creativity explodes into light.

Our culture seems bent on worshipping light and shunning darkness. Yet darkness is central to the earth's creativity. Her growth, the knitting together of her body, took place in the dark.

The sun was forming as a star and only began to burn and give light after the earth had begun to shape herself. It is the same in the womb. We grow and are formed in the warm dark as is the seed that must break open in the dark soil to create its flower and fruit. Life's way of birthing is everywhere. The images that are born in the dark are indeed "the future waiting to be born." My experience tells me that even though I do not understand or know what is happening as I change and grow, I can trust the creative process.

The earth is dying to her creative process because she is becoming so intoxicated by the poisonous wastes we empty into all her life systems. The earth is now the maiden in the fairy story, the creative one, the life-giving mother. The human seems bent on unwittingly selling this maiden to the Devil in exchange for riches and comfort. As we consume to live and live to consume, we cut off the earth's hands. We rob her of her ability to sustain life, we cripple her creativity. The tragedy is that what we do is so self-destructive. The creativity of this maiden, the earth, is our own. It is our radiance that we deny when we destroy hers. If she dies, we all die, life dies. If we cannot as a species begin to weep for the earth, to open to our feelings and express our sorrow and despair, we will not save the maiden from the devil we have created.

The earth has lost her fruitful relationship to the human, and the human has lost its fruitful relationship to God. The messages between us are intercepted by the Devil, who counsels death for profit. The price paid is the loss of the feminine and the destruction of the maiden, the earth, and her child, the human. If the human spirit can open to darkness and emptiness we can birth the images that we so desparately need. The image allows us to decipher the false messages and shows us how to draw on the wisdom of the mother so that we can save the earth from death. Learning to receive the wisdom of the mother means listening to the images from the "realm of the Mothers," from dreams and visions. It means taking the risk of birthing those images, trusting that they are "the future waiting to be born." The mother shows us the way to avoid destruction. The feminine within, with divine help, discovers "the place where all dwell free," the inner house where we learn how "to bring up the water of life from under the earth." The way of the mother is essential.

The story of creativity ends with a remarriage. Learning to bring together the separate parts of ourselves in love, and experiencing the remarriage of our wounded selves is powerful. As a species our task is to find the way to a remarriage with the lost feminine within our species, a remarriage with the lost feminine within the earth, and a remarriage with the lost feminine within God. Allowing the creative energies of both "the water of life" and the divine spirit to flow through us, sets us on the way to rediscovering the mother.

This rediscovery requires a recognition of our utter dependence on God and the life systems of the earth. It requires us to be willing to be small, to be emptied, to be hollowed out by pain, so that from that place of darkness, the light of creative change can erupt. As St. Paul describes Christ:

> He did not cling to his equality with God, but
> emptied himself to assume the condition of a slave.[6]

We, too, must empty ourselves to assume the condition of slaves to the unfolding power of creative love.

In the fairy tale, an angel always appears when the maiden cries out for help. In my experience, divine help is always there when I need it, as long as I do cry out. Crying out only happens when we have been willing to allow the unconscious images to speak in us. It is only imagination and longing, and tears and courage that save us from the Devil who waits to lure us away from the real way with promises of painlessly mined "gold." The cost of his false gold is always the same — the loss of the feminine, she who is in touch with feelings and creativity, she who can take risks and trust in the power of God and she who is pregnant with new life.

The Devil's false gold is purchased with denial. True gold is valuable only after it has been tested in the fiery furnace of reality. The human species stands poised to enter this furnace. Whether we will respond to reality and give ourselves to life's grand creative adventure remains to be seen. Yet we are rapidly reaching a place where reality will be thrust upon us, whether we can bear it or not. It is the reality of a dying planet. The words of St. Paul in his letter to the Romans take on a new meaning: "from the beginning until now the entire creation, as we know, has been groaning in one great act of giving birth."[7]

The future demands that we find ways to become participants in this great act of giving birth. The future demands that we respond creatively to the crises that face us as a species. The future demands that through our individual stories we discover the feminine, the Shekinah, and save her from the Devil. She is wandering in the wasteland of our hearts, and from there she longs to cry out for help. If we find her and allow her to speak, her cry will be heard by God. In the tender tension of that moment, we will discover as if for the first time, human hands tingling with divine creativity and healing love. Together with the divine Midwife, we shall bring the earth and all her creatures safely through the great act of giving birth.

CHAPTER SIX
Relationship
The Sharing of Love

The unrelated human being lacks wholeness, for he can achieve wholeness only through the soul, and the soul cannot exist without its other side, which is always found in a "You". Wholeness is a combination of I and You, and these show themselves to be parts of a transcendent unity whose nature can only be grasped symbolically, as in the symbols of the rotundum, the rose, the wheel or the conjunctio Solis et Lunae (the mystic marriage of sun and moon).[1]

Carl G. Jung

When the masculine is unbound, and the feminine is unveiled, then together they interact within and without. The penetrating power of conscious masculinity releases the eternal feminine. The woman awakens the man to his own receptive power. He penetrates her; she receives him. He awakens her to her own penetrating power; she awakens him to the presence of his own feminine soul. Together they are put in touch with their own inner wisdom. The process, not the goal, is all.[2]

Marion Woodman

For one human being to love another: that is perhaps the most difficult of all our tasks, the ultimate, the last test and proof, the work for which all other work is but preparation.[3]

Rainer Maria Rilke

She lay very still. Her breath was shallow. Each inhalation was painful. People filled the room. She felt as if she were surrounded by a warm cloak of love. Her life was complete. She could make her final journey in peace.

Flashes of old memories played before her. A child uncontrollably laughed as he tried to sing like a lark, but fell instead in a

86

heap of wet grass. She felt the fading warmth of her man's hand as she sat with him in his final hours. How she had missed him when he had first gone from her. She again felt the joy of his love, the abiding trust she had always known in him. She remembered the gentleness of his strong body, and the deep compassion he had shown for all living creatures. Now she could go to him again.

She had walked many strange roads, seen and heard things which could have made her mad. How little I have understood, she thought. Her mind took her back. Once more she was walking along the road under a cloudless sky. The harvest was full and birds sang everywhere. The smell of grapes hung in the air. She remembered it now like a dream. She had been consumed with her mission as she hurried along. The family was in agreement. Her son must be stopped. They knew of his words and actions. Her fear for him drove her forward. He had misunderstood. The strain of his life was affecting him. She must find him and bring him home to rest.

She had pleaded bitterly with him, using every maternal emotion she possessed to try to make him see reason. But it had been useless. She relived her feelings of abandonment. One of the women had run after her as she walked away in tears. Holding her in her arms, she had tried to comfort her, explaining gently that they could never fully understand him, they could only love him and let him live what was in his heart. Now that same woman, her namesake, sat at her bedside stroking her hand. How much they had shared since that time. Two women who knew the sweet pain of loving him completely. They had sat for hours in the dusky evenings talking and sharing stories of their love for him. Over and over she had repeated cherished memories from his childhood, polishing them like gems, while they laughed and held each other, delighting in his beauty. How different our lives had been, she reflected, yet our love for him united us. Mother and friend helping each other to keep loving when all seemed lost. They trusted together in the face of despair. She squeezed the woman's hand with the little strength she had left. It has been good to be together said the touch. Thank you for knowing my heart.

She felt herself drifting. She smiled and let herself fall. The darkness welcomed her like a friend and she gave herself willingly to this, her final journey. She had no fear. Love is stronger than death. The veil lifted and, for the first time, she knew him and understood.

* * *

The myth of Erich Neumann's *Amor and Psyche* is a powerful story of relationship. His commentary on this myth describes Psyche's journey as a woman in love, and her struggle to attain feminine consciousness. She achieves this through her love for Amor, or Eros. The myth describes her journey from the unconscious realm of darkness to the conscious realm of light. There is reason and choice and in the light she is able to make a commitment to her love for Amor. By insisting that she see her lover in the light and know who he really is, she wounds them both, and risks the death of the relationship. To quote Neumann,

> But it is this twofold wounding that first gives rise to love, whose striving it is to reunite what has been separated; it is this wounding that creates the possibility of an encounter, which is prerequisite for love between two individuals.[4]

By choosing consciousness, Psyche becomes free to choose her love for him and is able to commit herself to the task of recovering her lover and their relationship.

These tasks given to her by Aphrodite, her lover's mother, become her feminine heroic journey. The first three show how she unlocks the "knowledge-bringing masculine-positive forces of her nature." She must put order into "masculine promiscuity" by sorting the huge pile of seeds, find a way to avoid confrontation with "the overpowering masculine principle" symbolized by the raging rams, and finally contain the water from the stream that flows down the mountain, symbolizing the flow of life. In these three tasks, Psyche wrestles with the masculine principle and integrates it. In her fourth and final task she returns to the center of the matriarchal mysteries, journeying into the underworld of the unconscious, to confront the feminine power there.

On her journey into the underworld, she is cautioned strongly not to help the "weaving women" who will cry out to her. Neumann calls this the need for "resistance to pity." This is a powerful warning for the feminine journey. Psyche resists the pleas of the weaving women and is able to pass by all the obstacles placed on her path. She receives the gift of beauty from the goddess and returns to earth to deliver her hard won gift to Aphrodite. When she is safely back on earth's soil and close to the completion of her goal, she cannot resist opening the box she carries. Realizing that it will make her more beautiful, she impulsively decides to use it to help win back her lover. Because she steals the gift of the goddesses for herself, she is returned to a state of unconsciousness, a state of sleeping. This apparent failure becomes her ultimate success, because Amor is roused to come and save her.

> By preferring beauty to knowledge, she reunites herself, rather, with the feminine in her nature. And because she does this lovingly and for Eros (Amor), her old femininity enters into a new phase. It no longer consists in the self-contained beauty of a young girl who sees nothing beside herself, nor is it the seductive beauty of Aphrodite, who has only the "natural purpose" in mind. It is the beauty of a woman in love, who wishes to be beautiful for the beloved, for Eros, and for no one else.[5]

Psyche's surrender for the sake of love unveils her femininity and awakens Amor's masculine power to act, causing him to mature from a boy into a man. With his masculinity "unbound" and her femininity "unveiled," they become divine, and are married by the gods. Psyche gives birth to a divine feminine child whose name is Pleasure.

Like Psyche's my feminine journey leads me from unconscious girl into conscious woman. After Psyche had completed the tasks which helped her to develop a relationship to her inner masculinity, she faced the feminine power of the unconscious and brought her gift of beauty back into life. But once brought into the light of day, the gift must be surrendered for the sake of love. Only then can it be united with the masculine so that wholeness occurs. Psyche must return to her basic feminine nature — that which receives. By doing so, she embraces conscious femininity and motherhood. Without that surrender, a woman can become trapped in a masculine orientation towards life emphasizing doing rather than being, which destroys the feminine. Somehow the masculine way of action and penetration, and the feminine way of being and receptivity, must be united. This union requires a surrender, a willingness to die for love.

This myth speaks of the individual journey towards wholeness and the inner marriage of the masculine and feminine. Its wisdom also illuminates the outer marriage journey. I began my journey with little sense of my self, or my path. My love for Albert provided the catalyst for my inner work. My commitment to him was fundamental, but I had not really seen myself or my husband in the light of day. My relationship to an inner masculine figure is extremely wounded. I projected my need for that part of myself onto my husband. I gave him control over my life and, with it, responsibility for my happiness or lack of it. As the years go by, I am learning to withdraw my projections onto my husband and to perform the tasks necessary to allow the man within to emerge. In the beginning he was a hostile figure out to destroy me, but as I learn to face him, he is changing from a mean old man who keeps me helpless, to a source of strength and security.

One particularly vivid dream took place in a light and airy apartment. The room was large and breezes gently swayed the gossamer drapes at the windows. Comfortable cushions and sofas lined the walls. Beautiful tapestry rugs decorated the wooden floor. On the opposite side of the room was a beautiful black man. We were both naked. His eyes smiled at me with knowing love and I felt enveloped by his warmth. We had plans to go to the park for a picnic with my family, but we were both loathe to move. Being together was what mattered and the moment of recognition as we looked into each others' eyes made time stand still. I woke feeling the incredible love we shared.

Here is an image of the inner man. The connection I felt permitted me to trust him. There was no act to perform, no words to say, it was enough to simply be. Through his eyes I no longer was the "self-contained young girl" or "the seductive beauty," but rather a woman in love. I felt as though I have known this man all my life, though I have never seen him in waking life. He is my inner bridegroom.

My married relationship involves a spiral journey into my heart, searching for deeper levels of the freedom to give myself and the freedom to receive. There are many obstacles on the way. I want to remain a child, hoping that by doing so I will win the love I needed from my parents. I am afraid to choose a life of my own, fearing that I will not exist. I struggle with the responsibility for my life, knowing how difficult it is for me to accept myself and celebrate who I am. I find a myriad of ways to avoid being loved because it brings with it so much pain. At every stage of growth, however painful, a part of me fights to remain in illusion because it is what I know, rather than face the reality of the moment which is unknown and uncontrollable.

What emerges between Albert and me as we grow together is the belief that our healing and our wholeness takes place through, with, and in our love for each other. Our marriage is a safe place, a place where we can dare to be all of who we are. A place where we can share the blessed gift of laughter.

Our marriage is human. It fails us. We let each other down. We misunderstand each other, we wound each other, we feel hatred as well as love. To survive, it has been essential to ground our relationship in the love of a higher power, God. Surrendering our lives and the relationship to God is a daily experience. Thus, God guides and protects the marriage, strengthens it as sacrament, and deepens it as a divine as well as human bond. When my life and my love are given first to the deeper Mystery of existence, I am free to give myself to my husband and children. Prayer becomes my communion with all the daily tasks of life. Everything flows together and is charged with divinity.

Some days I feel that reality. Yet there are other days when I sabotage the chance for loving intimacy. Being loved at the center and letting another person into my heart is excrutiating. Yet I know it is the work of a relationship. I remember a time when we went away as a family for a weekend. Albert and Becky were sleeping in the car and I took Katie for a walk around the village. I kept telling myself what an enjoyable time I was having, reporting as if from outside myself on what I was doing. The inner truth was that I was lonely. I wanted to be with Albert. Later that night, I was able to tell him that — that I just love being with him, that I am most able to be myself with him. It felt as if the truth of my femininity was unveiled in that moment. Albert received my neediness and a new depth of intimacy was born.

Of course I cannot always be with him, but admitting the depth of the need in that moment without judgment creates freedom. It is the inner voice that needs expression, without silencing from the outer voices of what is "right" or "appropriate." I am a one time event of the earth, the solar system and the universe. My inner voice is neither right nor wrong. It is stating how I feel, and my feelings are always appropriate. By paying attention to them, my awareness of my deepest needs grows. The dream of an inner man happened after I began to accept my neediness.

Our marriage has not taken away my wounds. It has in many ways plunged me into them. I have not been able to make my husband love me in ways my mother or father could not. I have not been able to avoid my journey toward wholeness by loving my husband and daughters. Instead, the love I receive from them has allowed me to face the wounds and explore them, clean them out, and let them bleed. I wrote this poem after Katie's birth:

FOR ALBERT

Birth pains, rising and crashing
I want to bury myself in your skin
Hide my face in your strong, kind arms
Surrender to my need of you.

You are my life's midwife
The one who stands and knocks
Easing the openings of my heart.
Your love unlocks all my lonely secrets
Exposes all the bruises of my heart.

You know my empty spaces
The one who licks my wounds
Cleansing the rips in myself
Your tears soften all my shame-filled fears
Honor all the meanings of my soul.

Love grows, rising and crashing
I count the silver hairs in your beard
Each one a laughing memory.
I am at home in your great heart.[6]

Albert's response was a gift for our sixth wedding anniversary:

CAROL
We've seen the red bones of each other's souls.
We've visited the places where the heart
Bares its teeth and have picked its skin with a claw.

We've seen blood pour over our personalities.
But now it's spring again,
Matter unfolding from the night.
The raven opens a curved beak, biting at all the darkness.
Dawn, the pollen is in flight.
Our newborn baby is laughing.
We are face to face.
You cannot count the silver hairs in my beard.
Your eyes smile with a deeper kindness now.
Hands that have clutched, threatened, or pleaded
Are folded into rest.
Gulls spiral from a laughing sun.
What is this yearning in every cell of me?

What is this yearning for forms
That still cry from the dark and distant fire?
We are face to face.
My raging heart has bitten all the lips that hatred
And resentment can assume. My crumpled little self
Has softened and smiles with comfort now.
My blood has mixed with your blood;
Sparks from the ancient fire are one.

It's a real nice day to get married . . .

I think I'll marry you!⁷

To reach a place of trust where we can both be our "crumpled little selves," we have needed a commitment. We have needed a vow to God which is greater than us as individuals, so that when the two of us are broken and beaten we can go on walking because we are not in it for ourselves alone. The vow to a higher Mystery asks us to create a shared vision of our relationship, one that evolves as we do. What will we be together? What is our marriage for? How do I see you? How do you see me? When I met Albert, I saw his beauty, his goodness and his truth. I fell in love with my image of him. During many periods in our marriage he has not lived up to my image. He has become weak and despairing as he struggled with inner demons. I have had to believe stead-fastly in the original vision, knowing that the journey leads us to our deeper selves which will be born through love and patience.

It has been the same for him. The pretty, superficial girl he

married, who was so flattering and so devoted, has shown him
many ugly faces as she has changed from girl to woman. He has
had to hold fast to what he glimpsed in potential, while he
absorbed much of my pain and rage and stayed. I remember a
night when we both lay curled up in fetal positions sobbing
together at the knowledge of how much we had hurt each other.
The pain was paralyzing. We could offer each other no comfort.
We had no sense of whether healing was even possible. All we
had was the willingness to ache together. We could not have
gone there without a promise of fidelity.

Having a friend on the journey gives me the courage to open
the wounds and redeem the past. The core of the wound goes
back to my childhood. I believe that for women, and probably for
men too, all relationships ultimately lead us back to our mothers.
The relationship to father is essential too, but that would need
another book. In order to love and be loved in the present, I have
to find the way back to my mother and that first relationship, and
uncover the needs that were unmet. My deepest longing seems
to crystallize in the image of being taken in close to her body and
held; warm, safe and secure; loved and appreciated uncon-
ditionally. The beauty of the madonna and child icons and paint-
ings awaken that image over and over and help me to own it in
myself.

For me that first relationship of safety was damaged. I absorbed
my mother's terrible anxiety together with my own feelings of
terror, knowing that my life might be ripped out of her body
when it had hardly begun. I internalized a sense that I dare not
exist, that there was no safe place, that I could be totally abandoned at any time. The repressed pain of my mother's childhood
and her own unlived dreams created an underlying disappointment and unhappiness in her, which I assumed were caused by
me. I wasn't good enough. My mother was very ill during my
childhood. She would not let me or anyone else nurture her. I
had nothing of comfort to offer her. Slowly I internalized those
feelings and became unable to believe in myself. That spontaneous trust and joy in life and reality which we see in the total
acceptance of the mother and child images was not present, and
I have had to search within for the seeds of my own response to
life.

My mother and I have talked openly about these things. I do

not want to blame or criticize because I know intuitively that my mother mothered me much more lovingly than she herself was mothered. I know too that I am continuing some of the same patterns with my daughters because I am not yet conscious of them. These patterns go back for generations and can only be redeemed a piece at a time. The first step was to realize that I did not have what I needed internally, and that I could find ways to heal and choose life for myself. By entering that emptiness I am able to allow my inner values to grow and blossom, watered always by my love for myself and the love of other people. It is slow and difficult work, "perhaps the most difficult of all our tasks . . . the work for which all other work is but preparation." It is also the meaning of life.

For different reasons, many of our mothers were not able to provide us with the love we needed. Many of their own lives, like my mother's, were unfulfilled and they themselves were improperly loved. My own journey inward through the relationship with my mother has involved many feelings and stages. For a long time I idealized her, she was the perfect mother and I was the perfect child, but reality reared its ugly head and my illusions were shattered. For several years I was angry and hostile, painfully aware that the myth I believed was not emotionally true. My mother had not given me what I needed. I saw all the things that were missing and I lashed out as I licked my wounds.

Gradually I am becoming able to hurt honestly without the need to blame. I see my own responsibility in only internalizing the messages that confirmed my own sense of being inadequate. I confronted my mother, sometimes gently, and sometimes in a way that I know was devastating. With great courage she heard me, and during the worst of my rage and pain, she faithfully remained a part of my life. She came to help me at the births of my daughters. Those were tense days and she worked unceasingly to make things easy and smooth for me. With emotions running high, I know she had seriously considered whether to come at all. She taught me an important lesson about standing in the face of our children's criticism and not running away.

Recently, my mother visited me again. She had told me ahead of time that she was willing to share my feelings of anger and sadness and the struggle I was experiencing as I reclaimed my child self. I desparately wanted to share it with her but words did not seem enough, and often left us both feeling hurt and misunderstood. So I simply asked her if she would pray with me for healing of my terror in the womb. Together we asked for God's healing and I told her my story. We sobbed together about my fear of being killed. For the first time in my life I felt she heard me, and she held me saying over and over again "I would never kill you." We talked about her fear of her own father and her sorrow that she had not been able to stand up to him for me. In those moments I was closer to knowing my mother than ever before. Our woundedness connected us. I saw clearly her own inner child's wounding and we were at peace together, two vulnerable people who love each other.

The relationship with our mothers creates the primary model for our feminine selves. We are formed through, with, and in the body of mother and we will absorb the first messages about what our presence here means through her body. Our primary need is that she offer an unconditional place of safety and love. First, physically in the womb, and then emotionally and psychically, reaching outward in ever larger circles as we grow.

When my daughter Becky began school, I was struck by an image of circles that flow out from the mother. I could see the circles that embody the relationship of a mother to her child. There is the inner circle of the womb which gives way to a larger circle of the nursing infant, which enlarges to the larger circle of the toddler. There is no recognizable moment when one circle becomes another in those early years. But the first day of school seemed to signify the beginning of a larger world for Becky, a further stepping outward from the primary matrix. Her joyful steps further and further away depend significantly on her knowledge that I, her mother, remain firmly rooted in the center.

One afternoon Becky was playing badminton with her father and suddenly she said, "You know, Dad, when it comes to playing games, you're a lot more fun than Mummy, but when it comes to talking about things, Mummy's the best." Albert explained that he was always willing to talk with her about anything she needed to discuss, and she smiled and waved her racquet. "I know, Dad. I would talk to you," she said matter of factly, "if I didn't have a mother." In *Women and Choice*, Mary Rosera Joyce expresses Becky's knowing:

Because a woman can do what a father does, perhaps even better than some fathers, does not mean that she can be a father. And her children know it, even though they might not be able to explain it, and even though they might be taught how to deny it.[8]

The way of the mother is about making the journey back through life's circles, discovering myself in each of them, and loving the person I find there. I am fortunate enough to be able to return to the house I grew up in where my parents still live. One of the things I was able to do during a recent visit was to wander through each room, spending time allowing memories to arise of experiences I had while growing up there. Spontaneously my child or teenage self would appear in the room and I allowed myself to feel the feelings I had in that past moment, feelings which are still present because I could not express them then. I remember standing in my bedroom on the third floor of the house and seeing it as clearly as it was when I lived there as a teenager. My grandmother gave me fifty pounds when I was thirteen and I used it to decorate the room. The ceiling was painted a deep sea green and I chose a rug with shades of blues and greens to match. Printed phrases and sayings cut from magazines covered one wall. The small window gave me a view of the sea, and at night the wind would whip the waves into a frenzy and rattle the tiles on the roof. The pain of adolescence still seemed to cling to the walls and I felt a deep love for the structure of the house itself and for its shelter and space. I could see my dog sitting there with his head cocked making small whining noises because I was crying, and behind him the glass-topped desk which held my special poems and photographs sealed beneath the glass.

As I remembered I consciously embraced myself as I was then with all the acceptance and affirmation that I still long for. After spending some time in grateful prayer, I left the room bringing my teenage girl with me. I did this with each room in the house, as well as the garden where I had played so often with my sister and brothers. As I remembered, I reclaimed my past. The love I offered myself at every age experience was truly healing, and when I left the house I said a ritual goodbye, mentally gathering all of my childhood experiences. I felt that I was leaving home again, but that this time as I returned to my own home, I was not leaving part of myself behind.

That ritual helped me to move back through the circles of my life and the prayer with my mother in my home symbolized for me the way back into that primary circle. In those moments I met a mother who wants me, who loves me, who stands now at the center with arms outstretched ready to embrace me. She tells me now how she sees me as a friend, a woman, a mother and a daughter, and how proud she is of what she sees. She tells me that she loves me and that she will be with me forever. God gave us our own madonna and child experience. That connection enables me to let go of the necessary losses of the past. Making my way back to the center of that circle and finding my mother also frees me to walk away again.

Over time, my mother and I are establishing a different relationship. By honestly facing each other, we arrive at a common identity as women. We cannot always be there together. There are still wounds between us, and there are times when we both become defensive and victimized by each other. Yet the process is happening and I rejoice in it. My mother tells me that she feels better about herself today than she ever has. I have rediscovered my love and respect for her and a deep gratitude for the gift her body/soul has given me. I am aware of how much she has gifted me, as well as the empty spaces of what is missing. The feminine in myself that I treasure most was evoked by her way of being.

The past cannot be changed. It can only be accepted. Reclaiming the feelings from the past allows me to dwell in my center in the present and to allow my mother to dwell in hers. This frees us both from the negative embrace of dependency we shared for many years, one from which I had to escape, and allows us to choose to meet as individuals. Our love, however clumsy and imperfect, transforms us both. Recently I found a photograph my mother gave me of herself when she was four years old. Radiance and love flow from her face and in her eyes shines the openness and trust that the pain of her childhood years almost extinguished. There are many ways for all of us to meet, touch, and love each other. I am grateful to have met and to love the little child who is my mother.

I could not have made my way to my mother without first facing the negative mother whom I had internalized. The one who was depressed, who looked to me for her happiness, the one whom I could never finally please; the one who hated herself.

I had to see her in the light of day and free myself from her power. She convinced me that I was responsible for everything, especially others' happiness, and I stayed trapped in a cycle of failure and futility. Acknowledging that destructiveness and loving myself anyway frees me from her negative embrace, and allows me to discover her positive, creative energy. Hag was my negative mother, and as I love her and own her as part of me, she becomes transformed.

Everything that has taken place between my mother and me over the last ten years happened because I first discovered the wounds in my relationship with Albert. In this dynamic, I see and name my ugly self-destructive behaviors. It would have been easy for me to project my feelings on my husband and blame him, and I still do, but in the end I have to own my woundedness and take responsibility for my healing. Part of the mystery of our relationship has been that the acting out of my negative mother often triggers my husband's terror of his mother. Interactions like this between us will awaken childhood hurts from long ago. We have both needed to be willing to look at our own pain instead of blaming each other for the depth that is there. Thus our ugliness, our shadow selves, ultimately bring us gifts of healing; learning to trust and look for the gift behind the disguise is all part of a relationship.

One of the obstacles on my journey, which is an important one for me to be aware of, is the one Psyche confronts on her journey into the underworld. It is the pleas of the weaving women for help. Balancing my needs and the needs of others requires discernment. Sometimes I need to contain my love in order to follow my path. I need to be willing to surrender to my love of others at times. Creating the balance is a difficult and vital task.

During times of writing, I know that I need to create an inner tabernacle to contain the divine energy, so that I have fuel for my creative work. My tendency too often is to give my fire to others, thinking that it will light and protect their way, when in fact it is the oil that I need for my inner lamp. As the myth underscores, pity is not love and I need a resistance to making things easy for those I love by trying to take away their pain. I find this difficult with my children, knowing when to hold them close and when to let them walk their own path, resisting my need to make it easy for them.

The Gospel of Matthew contains a similar parable of warning.

Then the kingdom of heaven shall be compared to ten
maidens who took their lamps and went to meet the
bridegroom. Five of them were foolish, and five were
wise. For when the foolish took their lamps, they took
no oil with them; but the wise took flasks of oil with
their lamps. As the bridegroom was delayed, they all
slumbered and slept. But at midnight there was a cry,
"Behold, the bridegroom! Come out to meet him." Then
all those maidens rose and trimmed their lamps. And the
foolish said to the wise, "Give us some of your oil,
for our lamps are going out." But the wise replied,
"Perhaps there will not be enough for us and for you; go
rather to the dealers and buy for yourselves." And
while they went to buy, the bridegroom came, and those
who were ready went in with him to the marriage feast;
and the door was shut. Afterward the other maidens came
also, saying, "Lord, lord, open to us". But he replied
"Truly, I say to you, I do not know you." Watch
therefore for you know neither the day nor the hour."[9]

Taking responsibility for having what I need to fuel my life
requires great discernment. It means taking seriously my relationship to myself and to God. How often I am the foolish maiden
who responds unthinkingly to give to this one or comfort that
one, only to find that when I am finally alone and with myself, I
have nothing left, no fuel to burn my lamp. Instead of lovingly
greeting my bridegroom with my light, I can only sit exhausted
and empty. Knowing what allows me to keep my light burning —
my time in prayer, my creative time, my time with my husband
and children — I forsake them and rush off into some other task,
only to realize when I run out of energy, that I did not take the
time to "buy" the oil I need for my lamp.

Several years ago I began to write this book. The writing is my
journey into the mystery of the feminine; a way of travelling more
deeply into the unconscious realms to bring my own images of
the feminine back into the light of day. My changes have created
tension and change in the marriage, and we have had to constantly commit ourselves to feeling and talking things through,
acknowledging the pain of letting each other grow and the fear
that it causes each of us. We have both had to give up the illusion

of control of the other within the relationship. If the marriage is to be the joining of ourselves as one, then it must be the joining of people steeped in the mystery of the unknown, freely choosing to give themselves. As Albert's poem states "we are face to face." The early years of our relationship were certainly spent looking at each other, fascinated to learn everything we could about this other person. Slowly it seems our gaze shifts more and more toward God, toward our children, toward our life in the world, so that the journey becomes a way forward together, side by side.

This book is about the way of the mother. I began my journey with the love I feel for my husband. In the incarnation of that love I become a mother. I search for the way to a new relationship with my own mother. I find a relationship with my spiritual mother, whom I describe in the next chapter. I explore the way of the Great Mother, the world of the unconscious, through dreams and images. Finally I embrace the way of the primary symbol of the mother of us all, the earth. This is not a linear way where one path follows another, but a series of circular paths which I travel together, each deepening and expanding the others.

Once I was able to name and develop a relationship with God, my life changed. My images of God change too as I open my heart to divine intimacy. While it was relatively easy for me to relate to God the Father in my life I knew that I needed to find the feminine face of God both without and within me. Mary of Nazareth is a powerful and faithful guide for me as I search, but I know that God as Mother is infinitely greater than just the person of Mary. Now I see the earth as one of the symbols of God as Mother. The earth was created out of the primary Mystery, birthed from the dark "potential emptiness" of the Uncreated. The earth is impregnated by Light and she creates life. I am learning to see this Mother, to touch her, to be one with her. By loving her rich body, I can love my own. She grounds me physically in her earthy green Wisdom. She teaches me to honor my instincts, those gifts from her deep store of mystery, which I need for my survival. She roots me in the present moment and literally keeps my feet on the ground.

The earth's relationship with the sun is a symbol for me of the natural relationship of the masculine and feminine. Without the sun there would be no life on earth. Without the earth the sun's brilliance would shine without producing any living thing. Both are necessary. The dance between them is everything. Culturally we have worshipped sun gods. We still speak of God "up there" wherever that is. We long to be sun gods, brilliant, in control of the light, powerful and independent; mistresses and masters of all that lives. But we follow the purity of light at our peril, for alone it can bring us no life, no rich succulent roots. That is the earth's domain. It is she who waits, receiving the sun's rays, transforming them into life and nourishment, she who feeds us and gives us water. She is our home. She is the creation, the beauty, the richness, the diversity of our God. She mirrors God's face smiling on us with her gifts. So long as we stare blinded into the sun we shall not see her, and we shall miss so much of God.

All my relationships — with myself, with God, with Albert, with my children, my parents, my siblings and with my friends — are rooted in this primary dynamic of the earth and sun, of Mother and Father God. In their give and take they teach me how to love, how to give and how to receive, how to burn brightly with God's life and how to absorb that life and birth it anew. By discovering my love for the earth and hers for me, I feel at home, loved not only by a God who is Father both within and without, but also by a God who is Mother, who formed every cell of my body and who nourishes and delights in me.

This brings me to those first and most challenging relationships of my journey, those of mother to my own daughters. Each of the relationships I mention here prepares and teaches me how to be mother. Yet I know I fail. I love my daughters with a ferocity born from the knowledge of that failure. A love that would give them everything so that they will be whole and beautiful. But I am not perfect, nor will they be. They are different from me. The things that I try so hard to give them, which I did not have myself, will cast their own shadows. They have their own suffering. My hope when I reflect on myself as mother is simply to be there. To give my children my presence as a woman who lives from her own wounded center, who exalts in being alive, in being rooted in the earth, in sharing in the divine mystery, in being free to passionately love their father, in creating her own gift, in being their mother. My children have invited me to grow more than anyone else in my life. I am grateful to them and for them and if I give them nothing else, I pray that I can show them each their incredible beauty and dignity as daughters, sisters and mothers of God.

CHAPTER SEVEN

Wisdom
The Incarnation of Love

And so I prayed, and understanding was given me;
I entreated, and the spirit of Wisdom came to me.
I esteemed her more than sceptres and thrones;
compared with her I held riches as nothing.
I reckoned no priceless stone to be her peer,
for compared with her, all gold is a pinch of sand,
and beside her silver ranks as mud.
I loved her more than health or beauty,
preferred her to the light,
since her radiance never sleeps.
In her company all good things came to me,
at her hands riches not to be numbered.
All these I delighted in, since Wisdom brings them,
but as yet I did not know she was their mother.[1]
                    Book of Wisdom 7:7-12; The Jerusalem Bible

We may sum up the event thus far: the nature of God is love,
and the origin of love, the Father from whom is life, pours
himself out in total giving in the Beloved, who, in his human
nature, receives the outpouring of love, and receives it as
human, that is, as coinherent in all human life and in all creation.
Therefore (since sin is the condition in which created life is) he
receives it in a condition which 'blocks' the flow of love in
return. It is the work of incarnate Wisdom to make that longed-
for return possible.[2]
                                        Rosemary Haughton

The realization that a neurosis has a creative purpose applies
globally as well as personally, and surely, in an age addicted to
power and the acquisition of material possessions, the creative
purpose must have something to do with the one thing that can
save us — love for the earth, love for each other — the wisdom
of the Goddess. Responsibility belongs in the individual home,

103

in the individual heart, in the energy that holds atoms together
rather than blows them apart . . . .

When the Holy Spirit speaks, it can be terrifying because it
evokes profound fear of the unknown, fear of life, fear of stepping into our own destiny. If, however, men and women can
find their own virgin within, they can learn to Be, both alone
and with each other. The mystery lies in the possibility of Being.
Love chooses us.[3]

Marion Woodman

The woman seated at the bedside felt the life go forth from the
hand she held. She prayed fiercely, her head bowed over the frail
skin and bones. This was the flesh of his mother, the bones of
the woman she loved. She kissed each finger reverently and
withdrew from the room.

Slowly she made her way out over the fields, conscious of every
step she took, deliberately heading for a favorite spot of earth
where she could cherish her memories. She seated herself on the
warm soil and let her mind and heart open. The sun's rays
touched her skin. The grass tickled her feet. The rain had filled
each blade, and she pulled on a turgid root to suck the sweetness
from it. Many hours she had spent as a child in this way, alone
with the only mother she had known then, the mother of all
living things.

Memories of the dark craziness of her early life flooded through
her. And then the day when she first encountered the man whose
life and love had changed her so completely. Humiliated, trapped,
she tried to hide herself like a cornered animal. She heard his
footsteps amid the shouting voices and looked up defiantly. There
before her, shining in his eyes, was the love she had bartered for
her whole life. The tenderness her craven body longed for was
present in the touch of his hand. His gaze pierced her heart and
the aching need buried there came forth screaming. For an instant,
she hated him for stripping her so totally of her defenses. She
glared at him, every muscle tensed for the coming rejection. He
stood staring into the chasm of her emptiness, surveying her
ruins, all the dark secrets she had hidden away. He did not move.
She watched his eyes, waiting for the light in them to cloud over

with disgust, waiting for him to turn away. But the moment never came. His love continued to flow into her, and in his eyes she began to see the reflection of something beneath the inner rubble, a buried treasure glowing faintly in the darkness. He continued to look at her, inviting her to claim the gift as her own.

Her thoughts returned to the woman who had died. The woman whose love had given that man life. Without her motherly love she might never have been able to claim the gift her son had held out to her that day. It had been his mother, her namesake, who had healed so many of her body's wounds. All her life she had longed for a mother, for a mother's touch, for a mother's love. This woman had fulfilled her longing. So many times when the way had been hard, and she lay haunted by the ravaging lies of her old life, she had gone to her with her rage and her tears. Always there were strong arms to welcome her, a warm body to hold her close, a hand to wipe her hair. She had made her food, sat and listened, shared her struggle, been present to her with love. Now that body which had so grounded her was dead. Her wisdom was no longer present in living flesh.

She reached her arms to the sky and stretched her legs out in front of her, breathing in the pure air of a spring day. Life still poured through her limbs. Her love for this mother would never die. Each moment they had shared had taught her who she was, what her gift as a woman meant. Her soul would be nourished forever by their love. I shall never forget you, she whispered. I am a woman like you; I shall go forth, strong and loving, my heart filled with praise. Let it be done, she sang to the grass at her feet. Let it be done to me. Let me too be filled with the turgid sweetness from which all beings draw life.

*   *   *

One night I had a dream of my grandmother. She died some years ago from cancer. I had returned to England six months before her death, and although there was no knowledge of her illness at that time, I knew it was the last time I would see her. I spent several days at her home being with her, the two of us delighting in her meeting with Becky, her first great-grandchild. Some years after my grandfather's death, she had remarried. The marriage was touchingly happy for both of them. My grandmother's gratitude for the tender love of her final years was expressed again and again. She was a radiant seventy-year-old woman. The goodbyes when we left were painful. I promised her that I would always come if she needed me. We wrote several times during her illness, and spoke over the phone, but she did not ask for me to come, and as I was six thousand miles away, I did not go.

My grandmother was an important person in my life. I went to stay with her every year as a child, usually with my brother or sister. Every time I saw her, without fail, she would tell me the story of how she used to pray to live long enough to hear me talk. When I was a teenager, it used to irritate me to no end to hear those words again and again, but now they mean a great deal. In her living room, which was on the second floor, she had an old-fashioned cabinet with glass doors which were kept locked. In it were kept the "treasures." When I visited, she would take out an ornate key and as a special treat unlock the door and let me take out the toys and play with them. One was a little black hen that laid eggs at the pull of a string. I remember the preciousness of those things. How carefully I had to hold them. How special to be allowed to touch them.

In the dream I was sitting on her lap, in the same way that Becky, then nearly two, had done during our final visit. I was a grown woman. My grandmother was playing with my hands, laughing and delighting in me. Another woman was watching, and my grandmother was telling her that this was how she had played with me when I was a child. She was looking at me with such love that I was crying, a mixture of agony and joy at the depth of her love, and she too began to cry and we just looked into each other's eyes as we cried together. It was a recognition of all we meant to each other, all we had been and would be, and I awoke with a deep sense of comfort.

The following night I had another dream. In it I was a child in a courtroom, confronting my father for a crime he had committed against me. I feared that no one in this masculine court would believe me and I felt very small and insecure. The dream shifted, and I was walking with an older woman who had her arm around me. She told me that she knew that I was telling the truth and that my father had indeed wronged me. She told me that she loved me, and that it was okay, that I would be fine now.

On the third night, I dreamed I was wrestling with the question of suffering. I was trying to understand why life is often so difficult, and I awoke still hearing the voice of my mother speaking to me very tenderly. "This is the price you must pay for the fullness of life."

These dreams emerged in sequence. Each of them in a different way was telling me that I can now trust the feminine within. First, there was the wise old woman loving and being loved by me as both child and woman, and also showing me, the observer, that this was the way of love. She played particularly with my hands, singing and making games with my fingers. She thus showed me her delight in my creative powers and the importance of the play, as well as the work that springs from them. The second dream showed me another wise woman, this time affirming my wounded relationship to the father, the masculine within, the source of so much of my inner pain and struggle. Her validation of my child, her belief in my pain, was healing and integrating. She too affirmed the feminine way. Finally, as I struggled to make sense of all the pain and suffering involved in my quest for feminine spirit, my mother, the primary source, confirmed my way. The gentleness, the approval, and the pride in my accomplishment that was in her voice will always stay with me, reminding me that suffering is the way to the fullness of life, and that its price is always worth paying.

I experienced these dreams as the gift that I brought back from the underworld, the unconscious. Immediately after I received the gift, circumstances, both outer and inner, brought me to a point where I knew I had to make a deeper surrender in my love for my husband. It was a difficult movement within me in which I was being asked to exchange this newly found feminine spirit with my husband. I resented the promptings of my inner voice and wanted to keep the power for myself. I had worked hard to uncover this gift, and now I was afraid that by unveiling this deeper vunerability to Albert, I would lose the self I had gained. Perhaps to gain my life I must be willing to lose it in love.

I surrendered. Three days later, in my readings and reflections, I discovered the drawing by Leonardo da Vinci of St. Anne, Mary and the children Jesus and John. In the ink drawing, which is in The National Gallery in London, Mary is half-seated on the lap of her mother, Anne, holding Jesus, who is looking at the child

John, standing next to Anne. Simultaneously, Albert gave me the seed for the title of the book, by suggesting the word mother. I realized then that my initial dream of myself as both mother and child seated on my grandmother's knee was an archetypal symbol of the feminine. My individual inner portrait was unique, but the same fundamental symbol of wise woman, mother and child was there. I received it as my gift of feminine consciousness, revealed to me because of my willingness to give myself for the sake of love. What seemed at the time like a death of self in love was a necessary transformation to a deeper receptivity.

> Coming to wholeness requires receptivity. There is no
> wholeness without it. Receptivity is the beginning and
> continuous source of wholeness.[4]

If wisdom is the mother of all that is good, then wisdom is the reward of receptivity on the way of the mother. Wisdom is an elusive feminine spirit. She appears in myths and religions, and her disguises are many. Is it possible even to begin to articulate a way of discerning wisdom? There can only be hints and guesses at naming the feminine face of God, which we all search for, but which at best we only catch glimpses of.

Before wisdom appears, there are attitudes, ways of being that prepare me for her coming. The wise old woman, my grandmother in my dream, is one of the faces of the old crone, Hag, in my earlier dreams. She is becoming my friend, a wise woman who loves me, rather than a hateful hag whom I repress and reject. By loving and accepting her as part of myself, I allow her to become a guide. It is she who is now loving me, she who is celebrating my creativity and sharing her tears of joy with me. She would never have been redeemed without a long period of waiting. Receptive waiting is essential for opening the heart. It is a basic feminine stance toward life, however hidden it might become in an adoption of the masculine way of action and achievement. Physically, as a woman, I am always waiting — for my body to mature, for my blood to flow, for my body to conceive or not, for my child to grow within me, for the birth pangs to begin, for my milk to come in, and finally for my cycles of fertility to cease.

The story of the "Girl Without Hands" emphasizes the maiden's need to spend seven years in the forest waiting for her hands to grow back. Meditating on the mystery of the life of Mary of Nazareth speaks of this same truth. How long did she wait in prayer and longing before the Word was spoken and she conceived within her body? Or I ponder the months of waiting as her child grew within her. She must have doubted and questioned the mystery of all that was happening to her. A willingness to wait for life to unfold needs to be present for wisdom to reveal herself.

Within the waiting, there grows a desire, a longing to receive wisdom. Receptivity is an active attitude, not a passive one. It requires openness and trust. Trust deepens as I look back over my journey and see that I have received wisdom along the way. This mother has led me forward and with purpose, regardless of the monsters and obstacles I have met on the way. I remember a time after years of preparing myself, actively pursuing growth, when I seemed to hit a brick wall and could go no further with the process. I knew there was still a deep wound internally, and I felt a real sense of futility for nothing seemed to take it away. In desperation, I began to meditate and to spend time each day sitting quietly, waiting and trusting in the love of God. I stopped trying to control my growth, or to make it happen, or even to understand it. As I continue to wait this way, I trust the mystery of the healing I know is taking place. All my efforts were not working. I cannot fix myself; I simply have to be myself. The wound is me and within the wound I find the love of God.

Waiting, trusting, desiring all lead to listening. Listening is an art. How much easier to talk, to analyze, to understand. Real growth takes place when I learn to listen. Listening helps me to become receptive; receptivity helps me to listen. Accepting that the way, the next step, is unknown helps me to trust. Thus, I wait, I trust, and I listen. I think of the story of Martha and Mary in the Gospel, the two sisters who were so close to Jesus. When he was visiting their house for a meal, Martha was busy with all the preparations and the serving, while Mary sat listening to Jesus talk. Martha grew resentful and finally asked Jesus to tell Mary to help her, but Jesus refused, saying that it was Mary who "had chosen the better part," and that it would not be taken from her. Mary and Martha exist in my heart, and their needs are often conflicting. There is a beauty in serving and caring for others, but there is also a beauty in sitting quietly and listening for the words of wisdom.

We all struggle to articulate what life means. Often during the painful and difficult inner work on my heart I longed to discover a calling to do something important. Take a job, begin a career, go back to school. I spent enormous amounts of energy trying to discern what it was I should be DOING, what would make me happy, convinced that there was some role that would make life more meaningful and make me okay. When I was able to still my frantic mind and become receptive to God, a small voice inside counseled me to BE a mother. It seemed so insignificant and undramatic. It also terrified me, because I felt and still often feel so ill-equipped to mother. It requires that step into the unknown. That voice has never changed, however many different ideas and schemes I have thought up. My inner wisdom counsels mothering, counsels BEING, not doing, and I have slowly come to see that a way that I thought was limiting and unexciting, once embarked upon, is becoming ever richer and more meaningful. God as wisdom speaks to me as mother, and at last I am learning that following her call leads me to my greatest personal fulfillment and also to my rightful place in the whole.

The inner image of the three feminine figures, wise woman, mother, and child was only given to me toward the end of this book. By trusting wisdom's voice I am being led more deeply into the mystery of the mother. It is not the way of the mother that is limiting, but my understanding of the path. As I open my heart and expand my capacity to love, so do I expand the ways of interpreting my life as mother. The earth is mother; why should I desire to be other than she from whom I spring?

Experience tells me that to find wisdom I need not actively search. My task is to focus my desire to receive her words with an open heart; to wait, to trust, to listen, and to be still. Wisdom speaks in the language of simplicity. It is easy, therefore, to dismiss her voice, because it seems so unsophisticated or impractical. Her ways are not complex or necessarily exciting. Wisdom reveals herself in the simple truth of the heart's deepest longing. Moments when I am suddenly aware that I am speaking from a place of inner truth, and that as I speak the words, I hear and know them for the first time, are experiences of wisdom. Statements that I make at those times are always deceptively simple.

It has taken me a long time to learn to speak them and not to reject them. To many people they sound ridiculously naive, but they prove to be the very teaching needed in the moment. As women we need to learn to articulate those inner voices so that we may bring their words to wisdom's store.

Wisdom's store is rich. It is different from knowledge. An obsession with knowing, with analyzing, with figuring it out causes my mind and heart to speed up and I feel anxious. The culture seems obsessed in the same way. Life becomes a frantic racing from one activity to the next, gathering huge amounts of knowledge, filling our minds with ideas and concepts, while our hearts atrophy, and the store of wisdom in our culture diminishes. Wisdom is feminine; she is mother. She comes to us out of the depths of our feminine selves, and we have a responsibility to speak the wisdom which comes to us in the hope that her store will not disappear. The source of wisdom is ancient and deep, but her flowing is suffocated by superficiality and intellectual mind games. As I slow down and open my heart to receive the spirit of wisdom, my life changes and simplifies. Surely this is what the earth needs more than anything for us as humans to live simply.

Wisdom is humble. Her words are never haughty or self-aggrandizing. T. S. Eliot wrote in "Four Quartets" that humility is the only wisdom we can hope for because "humility is endless."

The wise person is humble. Humility is an attitude of openness, of vulnerability, of being willing not to know. When I am humble I can be shown my rightful place in the cosmos, a place close to the earth (humus), where I can see myself as I really am, good and evil, taken together. I can recognize the larger movement of life in which I exist and accept my smallness in the face of the awesome power of the emerging universe process. This humility is indeed endless, because it centers my attention on who I am in relationship to the whole, so that all I am and do and hope is held within the larger wisdom of God. It allows me to recognize that every being shares in this wisdom and can reveal its being to me if I am open. The wisdom of the whole universe can indeed be glimpsed in a grain of sand or a drop of water.

Wisdom is gentle and contemplative. She does not coerce or bully, nor does she protect from the sting of truth. She shows me the way but does not insist I walk it. In so many ways she is the mother who smiles lovingly upon me, tells me how to walk and then trusts me as I stumble forward, ready to sit me on her lap if I fall. Wisdom is the loving mother which our world so desperately needs to give birth to. As the way of the mother spirals in and out, I imagine circles moving outward from her source like ripples in a pond. My way is to journey back toward the center, sometimes flying, sometimes diving, always stumbling. In that center I find myself in a new way but also something much greater. Here is the ancient mother of us all, she who has been present since the beginning.

If wisdom is the ancient mother, or grandmother, of the feminine way, it is Mary of Nazareth who guides me as mother on the spiritual journey. It is she, a strong, loving woman that she was and is, who quietly reveals wisdom to me. She is a woman misunderstood today. Many of the images of her contain masculine projections and interpretations of who she is as a woman and a mother. Thus many women reject her as an impossibly unrealistic guide. My experience is to look into the heart of the woman, Mary, stripped of all her titles and robes, to sit and wonder about her life, her gift for the whole, and her attitude toward it. She teaches me well. She was and is a woman who made a difference; someone who sensed the incredible pain of her world and offered herself as an instrument of hope and change; a woman who embraced suffering, ridicule, misunderstanding, and constant change in her life, with a trust and a love which echoes throughout time. She longed for wisdom, she waited, she trusted, she heard Wisdom's voice, and she gave herself totally in response to it. She birthed God, bleeding her Son forth in a stable. Her being is the being of a woman who actively received Life in love, who trusted the inner voice and not the outer reality, who opened her heart to be pierced, knowing it was the price for the fullness of life.

In her beautiful poem, "Magnificat of Waiting for the Fullness of Time," Ann Johnson speaks for Mary with words for all who wait in hope for the coming of wisdom and new birth:

My soul reflects quietly on your fullness,
and my spirit grows stronger in the hope of your promise,
God my redeemer, because you have filled me with the
knowing that you are alive within me.
Yes, day by day through the course of time

my awareness of the call to blessed fulfillment increases
for you have done great things in me.

Holy is this time,
and patience is your gift
to all who nurture the seed of your love.
You have changed my life;
I was so confident in my unknowing.
You have deflected my fervent thrust toward iron-clad goals,
and spread before me your vision of fragile simplicity.
My longing to be a healing and reconciling person to your people
is affirmed within the daily comings and goings of my life;
my illusions of my own wholeness are mercifully revealed.
You are here now in this seeming emptiness of waiting.
remembering your intent,
. . . according to the promise made in the beginning of time . . .
remembering your intent to reach through the work of my life
that your fullness may be known now, in our time.[5]

In *The Passionate God*, Rosemary Haughton describes the relationship between wisdom and the human, using Mary as "the medium of exchange":

But in the transition from the gracious self-gift of Wisdom to the uttermost extreme of passionate sacrifice there has to be a "medium of exchange." There has to be flesh, human being; but Love does not "take" body, it requests it, it avows neediness, it waits upon the reply of the beloved. And this cannot be a generalized one; again, there is need of the particular response. Mary's fiat is indeed the response of creation to its Lover, but it is that because it is her own, her personal and unique response of love . . . But she is not merely passive, hers also is *amour voulu*, a willed and conscious co-operation in the work of recreation . . .

Mary is the "handmaid," the slave of the Lord, she is one of the poor . . . . She is earth, body, "medium of exchange," yet she is all three (because otherwise she could not be these) as conscious and fully willed, as active and sensitive, as a real human life. It happens because of a real woman's courage and doubt and joy and bewilderment and deep pain and utter fidelity.[6]

Mary is the virgin who reveals my inner virgin, the soul's space where I can learn to say Yes to Life and to embrace Being. Mary, as earth, received the Word of Wisdom completely. She responded to the voice who called to her with the words: "How

can this come about?" Yet she faced her fear and walked forward
into her destiny. The way of the mother is the way of the virgin
Mary, the mother of God, the daughter of earth. Mary of Nazareth
is the mother, who when I falter with fear at the words spoken
at my own annunciations, whispers her encouragement.

Mary embodies as human being, as earth, the feminine spirit
of wisdom. Psychologically, the sphere of the feminine unconscious has been named The Great Mother. Eric Neumann, in his
book entitled *The Great Mother*, articulates a symbolic represen-
tation of this realm.[7] Demeter, Sophia, and Wisdom become Mary,
Mother, and Virgin in the realm of the good mother and the
positive feminine. They are the figures who are embraced on the
way of the mother. But there are also the negative feminine figures, Astarte and Hecate, representing the terrible mother, the
young witch and the old witch. These figures must also be inte-
grated into the psyche on the way of the mother. My experience
with Hag was for me the embracing of the terrible mother, the
witch who would trick me into feeling lost and helpless, unable
to commit myself because she made me believe that my mother
did not love me. Befriending her and allowing myself to feel and
express her anger and her pain has allowed me to find Mary
within myself too, but both are always present.

The Great Mother images spring from the unconscious realms
of the psyche which are common to all of us, male or female.
Another way for me to name this unconscious realm is to call her
the earth, the deep feminine. The earth is a psychic and a physical
reality; she has a mind and a body. In the deepest realms of our
selves, both psychically and physically, the earth represents the
good mother. The earth can be seen as the collective unconscious
of which Carl Jung spoke. She is a zone of the psyche which is
shared by all the members of the life community. The way of the
mother is also the way of the earth; a new way to see her, to
appreciate her, to feel my deep historical roots. I am woman, she
who springs from the earth, who partakes in the richness of
history, both pre-human and human. My roots, both physically
and psychically, are deep in the soil, the waters, and the air.

Once in touch with those roots, there is a sense of the divinity
of the earth process. The earth is not only the Creation of God,
but also the Creator; seeded by God, but also birthing God. From
her soils come also all the symbols of my faith. Integral to my

own journey is the gift of the Eucharist, and I meditate constantly on the words of Jesus, "Take eat, this is my Body, which is given for you." The inner nurturing that His Body gives me opens my heart to the reality that those words are spoken everywhere. As the universe began in one tremendous explosion of light and heat, God's voice echoes, "Take eat this is my Body, which is given for you." As the earth unfolded and gave herself as food to countless life forms, the words resonate again, and each time she offers water or food or clothing, the earth whispers "Take eat, this is my Body."

It is this wisdom of the entire universe which is present in my motherhood. When I am with child, I too must speak the same words, "Take eat, this is my Body, which is given for you" to this new life. As I feed her from my breast, the words echo again within me. How beautiful and mysterious that a human child is able to blossom and grow on only the food my body provides. How wise my body is. How awesome and mysterious is the earth's ability to offer me her Body to eat so that I can offer my body to my child. The earth feeds all life, including each of us, from her Body. How wise her Body is.

When my child leaves and begins her journey in the world, I will hear those words as I send her forth: "Take eat, this is my Body, which is given for you." Here she is; may she be food for a hungry world, a world in great need of her feminine spirit. As it is with my physical and biological gift, so it is psychologically. Each time a moment of grace births a new movement toward wholeness within me, I incarnate the gift and offer it to others as food. I have birthed and nurtured the words on these pages and now I need to send them forth. They are my spirit's flesh and bones and I falter with my offering, wanting to protect and hold on to it, as I sense I shall want to do with my children. Ultimately, it is only crucifixion that transforms us into food.

The more I reflect on this central mystery of "take eat, this is my Body," the more I understand the pattern. Jesus knew Life's pattern, His Father had seeded it, and His Mother had birthed it, and because He knew that the process worked, that it gave life, He chose to leave the pattern of their creation for us. Jesus loved the earth; his love is present in the stories he told his followers. He longs to bring the human person and the whole of creation to wholeness. What He saw everywhere on the physical level, He incarnated on the spiritual level. He feeds us with the fruit of the Earth process — matter — and He feeds us with the transmission of divine spiritual power in the Eucharist — spirit — and it is not separate, but a unity of the two. It is not either matter or spirit, either Mother or Father, but both matter and spirit, both Mother and Father, and the whole is greater than the sum of the parts, and it is a w-holy mystery, and it is a deep blessing. Through his death on the cross He set in motion the saving redemption that the entire creation has been groaning to give birth to. He comes to restore the original gift of Love that was lost.

As I ponder the loss of feminine values in so much of our culture, and especially the struggles of women in the Church, it is good for me to remember that all the gifts of my faith emerge ultimately from a feminine source. Jesus was birthed by a woman, his Mother. The altar of sacrifice is in the center of "Holy Mother Church," and we enter her womb in order to receive the seed which brings life. The bread and wine that become sacred food are birthed by the feminine Body of the Earth, our Mother. The unbroken unfolding of evolution from the first gift of Light was birthed from the dark womb that pre-existed the Word. Every life form since the beginning has been birthed out of the uncreated potential of God. The feminine dimension of God receives the seed of the masculine dimension of God, transforms it, and brings it into being. The masculine is contained within the feminine. The mother births the father; both are necessary for wholeness. This is the wisdom I need to claim as a woman: to stand and find ways to value my magnificent creative power; to see all beings as springing from this feminine reality and from that inner knowing, to birth the symbols which can bring to our rituals the feminine dimension of God; to search for an answer to the question, "What rituals and symbol would a feminine priestess use?" rather than to argue about whether there should be female priests.

Courage is needed to express the rage that comes from the ways the feminine is being misused and controlled, but the rage cannot be misdirected in an attitude of blame. It is only in taking responsibility for birthing the feminine that any answer lies. Exhausting energy in blaming allows me to remain a victim. Real change requires a positive vision from within my self, not a negative attack on what is without. The dance between the masculine and the feminine has clearly become unbalanced, but the dance can and must become a celebration again. The dance steps will only be learned by listening to the wisdom of the dance of Being as it is, and not in recreating them as they "should" be. The human is not the "lord of the dance," but only a joyful participant in Life's ancient rituals.

God is the seed of life which is Light, and God is the process of the Earth, receiving and containing the seed, and through that exchange of love, the seed grows and bears fruit. The earth journeys slowly around the sun, receives its rays, and brings forth Life; Mary journeyed, received the love of God, and brought forth Life. I too journey, receiving the love of my husband in the sacredness of my vow to God so that I can bring forth Life. There is no separation; it is one process of divine Love unfolding.

I share this small poem, whose author is unknown to me. Its message speaks directly to my way:

> The earth woman wears a necklace of corn;
> Her body is a planted field, a reaping ground;
> "Learn," she says, "the patient way of seeds.

I need to stand in my femininity as a woman of the earth. I need to learn the patience of seeds, the cycles of birth, death, and rebirth which are the cycles of the Mother. I need to offer myself as a "reaping ground" from which many may gather food.

The way of the Mother is the way home. We all need mothers. We cannot be born without them, and we cannot be reborn again and again without the deep sense that we are mothered. That is the way of the Mother: to be a participant in birthing and nurturing new life, physically, psychically, and spiritually. Now within my heart I see the blue-green earth, and on her lap sits Wisdom, her daughter Mary, my grandmother, my mother, myself, my daughters, all women, sprung from the womb with loving arms outstretched. The feminine spirit of mothering is for us all, men and women both. She is the spirit of wisdom, of compassion, of healing, the one who feeds us all with her Body. She is speaking powerfully today, begging us to acknowledge her, to learn to see her again, to discover the way of the mother.

For when, as a culture, we find the Mother with all her many faces, as wisdom, as Mary, as the earth, as the unconscious, as our own mothers, and as a part of ourselves, we discover that we are no longer orphans. Our source is no longer either the

Christian Father in heaven or the Native Mother Earth, but in a
joining of the two. If the marriage of the masculine God as symbolized by Father, Creator, Sun and the feminine Goddess as symbolized by Mother, Wisdom, Earth takes place, we can afford to
become children, to fall in love, to trust, to hope, and to begin
the difficult work of creating the kingdom, teaching our species
the truth of how we can live together, loving the earth and loving
one another as family, daughters and sons of the same Father
and Mother, whom we cannot live without.

> The capacity for motherhood is the source of women's power but
> also of their vulnerability. A woman can bear children but she can
> also be raped. It is this very combination of power and vulnerability
> that Jesus called on in the women he encountered. Most of them
> were mothers, yet in his eyes they were not determined by their
> motherhood, neither were they required to reject it. In their experi-
> ence of being capable of motherhood these women discovered the
> power to use the qualities of motherhood in mission.
>
> Women, now, need to rediscover the power of motherhood, and
> to claim it as a liberating power. Whether or not they bear children
> in their bodies they are called to bear a new world to birth, if there
> is to be one at all.[8]

Each one of us is an essential participant. The way of the mother
dares not remain the lost journey of the feminine. Responsibility
for the way does belong in the individual home and in the individual heart. None of us can ultimately escape our terrifying and
wonderful destiny. "Love chooses us," and when we hear the
voice of Wisdom, we need only say with Mary, "I am the handmaid of the Lord . . . (I am the daughter of the Earth) . . . let
what you have said be done to me." Yes, I will become mother
to your divine life. Yes, I will bear a new world to birth. In that
moment of mystery, in the terror and the ecstacy of each conscious
"Yes," lies the promise and the possibility of the future.

Epilogue

Capturing in words the ideas, images and relationships that are embraced on the way of the mother is an arduous task. Words like masculine and feminine, mother and father, tend to be so overused and divisive that they create separate realities, rather than point to the wholeness within which both exist. Yet I believe the lack of wholeness in our lives is due to the loss of relationship with the Mother in so many ways. It has taken me weeks, months and years of work to say what I have said here. While I know what I mean, I am still aware that for you the reader, my words may be unclear and paradoxical. So, I would like to leave it to a child to give the last word.

After weeks of editing under a deadline from the publisher I came to the final chapter, Wisdom, and decided to wait one more day to complete the work. Albert had made supper and we were all in the kitchen talking and laughing. I turned to Katie and told her that I wanted her to get ready for bed while I did the dishes. "Okay, but you will put me to bed, right, Mummy?" Albert responded immediately, "What's wrong with Daddy putting you to bed?" Becky walked over, put her hand on his shoulder and said emphatically, "She's our mother. We lived in her."

The wisdom in that moment stunned both Albert and me. Perhaps I have spent the last years trying to say what Becky articulated in a few seconds. The mother is she whom we live in, psychologically, physically and spiritually. She births us, she nourishes us, she is the ground from which everything grows. If we are to survive as a species it is essential that we know what Becky knows, in our relationship to the earth. "She's our mother. We live in her."

Notes

PREFACE

1. Muriel Rukeyser, "Kathe Kollwitz" from *No More Masks*, Howe & Bass, eds., (New York: Doubleday/Anchor Books, 1973) p.103.

INTRODUCTION

1. Thomas Berry, *The Dream of the Earth* (San Francisco: Sierra Club Books, 1988) pp.211, 215.
2. Anthony Stevens, *Archetypes: A Natural History of the Self* (New York: William Morrow & Co., 1982) p.85.
3. Mary Rosera Joyce, *New Dynamics in Sexual Love* (Minnesota: St. John's University Press, 1970) p.59 — out of print.

CHAPTER ONE – BIRTH

1. Stephanie Demetrakopoulos, *Listening to Our Bodies: The Rebirth of Feminine Wisdom* (Boston: Beacon Press, 1983) p.24.
2. Marion Woodman, *Addiction to Perfection: The Still Unravished Bride* (Toronto: Inner City Books, 1982) p.125.
3. Albert LaChance, "Jonah Poem #8", unpublished.
4. Albert LaChance, "Carol at Rebecca's Birth," unpublished.
5. Pablo Neruda, *Twenty Love Poems & A Song of Despair*, translated by W.S. Merwin (New York: Penguin Books Ltd., 1969) p.43.
6. Mary Rosera Joyce, *Women and Choice: A New Beginning* (St.Cloud, Minnesota: LifeCom, 1986) p.165.
7. Brian Swimme, *The Universe is a Green Dragon* (Santa Fe, New Mexico: Bear & Co., 1985) p.58.

CHAPTER TWO – BEAUTY

1. Linda Schierse Leonard, *On the Way to the Wedding: Transforming the Love Relationship* (Boston: Shambhala, 1987) p.173.
2. John Keats, "Endymion" from *Complete Poems of Keats and Shelley* (New York: Random House, Inc./The Modern Library).
3. Brian Swimme, "The Evolutionary Cosmos," Graduate Course at Institute of Culture and Creation Spirituality, Holy Names College, Oakland, California, 1984.
4. Murray Bodo, *Clare: A Light in the Garden* (Cincinnati: St. Anthony Messenger Press, 1979) p.14.
5. Ellen Bass, "Tampons," *Chrysalis* (Fall 1979) pp.47-49 from *Listening to Our Bodies: The Rebirth of Feminine Wisdom* (Boston: Beacon Press, 1983) p. 24.
6. Joanna Rogers Macy, *Despair and Personal Power in the Nuclear Age* (Philadelphia: New Society Publishers, 1983) p. 30.
7. Morris West, *The Clowns of God* (New York: William Morrow & Co. Inc., 1981) p.366.

CHAPTER THREE – TERROR

1. Rainer Maria Rilke, *Letters to a Young Poet*, translated by M.D. Herter Norton (New York: W.W. Norton & Co., 1963) p.69.
2. Marion Woodman, *Addiction to Perfection: The Still Unravished Bride* (Toronto: Inner City Books, 1982) p.26.
3. *The Jerusalem Bible*, Psalm 139:13-15 (New York: Doubleday & Co. Inc., 1966) p.922.
4. Anthony Stevens, *Archetypes: A Natural History of the Self*. See Chapter 7, esp. pp.96-97.
5. Suzanne Noffke, editor, *The Prayers of Catherine of Siena* (New York: Paulist Press, 1983) p.18.
6. *The Jerusalem Bible*, Isaiah 29:18, p.1188.
7. For further information see Albert LaChance, *Greenspirit: Twelve Steps in Ecological Spirituality, An Individual, Cultural and Planetary Therapy* (Rockport, Mass.: Element Books, 1991).

CHAPTER FOUR – DEATH

1. *The Jerusalem Bible* Book of Deuteronomy 30:19-20 (New York: Doubleday & Co. Inc., 1966) p.255.
2. Linda Schierse Leonard, *On the Way to the Wedding*, p.140.
3. Stephen Levine, *Meetings at the Edge: Dialogues with the Grieving and the Dying, the Healing and the Healed* (New York: Doubleday & Co. Inc., Anchor Press, 1984) p.xiv.
4. Grimm Brothers, *The Complete Grimm's Fairy Tales* (New York: Pantheon Books, 1944, 1972) p.20.
5. Walter Brueggemann, *The Prophetic Imagination* (Philadelphia: Fortress Press, 1978) pp.112-113.
6. Ibid.

CHAPTER FIVE – CREATIVITY

1. Carl G. Jung, *The Collected Works* Vol. 15 (Princeton, N.J.: Princeton Univ. Press, Bollingen Series XX, 1966) p.103.
2. Rainer Maria Rilke, *Letters to a Young Poet* Letter #3 quoted in Matthew Fox's *Original Blessing* (Santa Fe, N.M.: Bear & Co., 1983) p.201.
3. Helen M. Luke, *Woman, Earth and Spirit: The Feminine in Symbol and Myth* (New York: Crossroad, 1987) p.3.
4. Grimm Brothers *The Complete Grimm's Fairy Tales* (New York: Pantheon Books).
5. Carol LaChance, "Sister," unpublished poem.
6. *The Jerusalem Bible, New Testament* Philippians 2:6-7, p.340.
7. *The Jerusalem Bible, New Testament* Romans 8:22, p.280.

CHAPTER SIX – RELATIONSHIP

1. Carl G. Jung, *The Psychology of the Transference* (Princeton, N.J.: Princeton University Press, 1971) pp.82-83.
2. Marion Woodman, *The Pregnant Virgin: A Process of Psychological Transformation* (Toronto, Canada: Inner City Books, 1985) p.170.
3. Rainer Maria Rilke, *Letters to a Young Poet*, pp.53-54.
4. Erich Neumann, *Amor & Psyche: The Psychic Development of the*

Feminine (New York: Princeton University Press, Bollingen Series LIV, 1956) pp.85-86.
5. Ibid., p.123.
6. Carol LaChance, "For Albert," unpublished poem.
7. Albert LaChance, "For Carol," unpublished poem.
8. Mary Rosera Joyce, *Women and Choice*, p.181.
9. *The Jerusalem Bible, New Testament* The Gospel of Matthew 25:1-13, p.56.

CHAPTER SEVEN – WISDOM

1. *The Jerusalem Bible* Book of Wisdom 7:7-12, p.1014.
2. Rosemary Haughton, *The Passionate God* (New York/Ramsey: Paulist Press, 1981) p.153.
3. Marion Woodman, *The Pregnant Virgin*, pp.139, 169.
4. Mary Rosera Joyce, *Women and Choice*, p.153.
5. Ann Johnson, *Miryam of Nazareth* (Notre Dame, Indiana: Ave Maria Press, 1984) p. 79.
6. Rosemary Haughton, *The Passionate God*, pp.139-140.
7. Erich Neumann, *The Great Mother* (Princeton, N.J.: Princeton University Press Bollingen Series XLVII, 1955) p.83.
8. Rosemary Haughton, *The Re-Creation of Eve* (Springfield, Illinois: Templegate Publishers, 1985) p.146.